CHANGING the GAME

CHANGING the GAME

Strategies for
*LIFE, BUSINESS, AND
THE PRACTICE OF LAW*

DARREN A. MILLER

Advantage | Books

Published by Advantage, Charleston, South Carolina.
Member of Advantage Media Group.

ADVANTAGE is a registered trademark, and the Advantage colophon is a trademark of Advantage Media Group, Inc.

Printed in the United States of America.

10 9 8 7 6 5 4 3 2 1

ISBN: 978-1-64225-175-3 (Hardcover)
ISBN: 978-1-64225-451-8 (eBook)

LCCN: 2022917706

Book design by Wesley Strickland.

This publication is designed to provide accurate and authoritative information in regard to the subject matter covered. It is sold with the understanding that the publisher is not engaged in rendering legal, accounting, or other professional services. If legal advice or other expert assistance is required, the services of a competent professional person should be sought.

Advantage Media Group is a publisher of business, self-improvement, and professional development books and online learning. We help entrepreneurs, business leaders, and professionals share their Stories, Passion, and Knowledge to help others Learn & Grow. Do you have a manuscript or book idea that you would like us to consider for publishing? Please visit **advantagefamily.com**.

This book is dedicated to my beautiful wife, Comfort.
No one has sacrificed more in our lives over the last twenty-five years
than her. She has provided me with counsel, love, and support, always
putting her needs behind the needs of others. To this day, when I have
a problem that needs to be solved, she is the first person I turn to in
order to help me reach the right decision. Thank you for everything,
my love. I look forward to the next twenty-five years with you.

CONTENTS

THE GAME CHANGER

How can I help you?

You'd be hard pressed to find a more powerful phrase in the whole English language than those five simple words. Consider how often, in how many different ways and how many different places, that phrase is lobbed at strangers every day.

You approach the counter at the DMV and these words immediately greet you: "How can I help you?" You shuffle your way to the front of the line to order a burger or a burrito, and what do you hear? "How can I help you?" You stroll into a lawyer's office and scoot yourself into a chair opposite some expansive desk in the back of a corner office, and an attorney says to you, "How can I help you?"

Maybe it's a phrase that's become a casualty of its own ubiquity. Perhaps its shine has lost some of its luster due to overuse and the fact that the vast majority of people who ask the question "How can I help you?" really mean something different altogether.

1

What they're really asking is some variation of the more pedestrian question, "What do you want?"

If you're motivated to become a better lawyer—a better mass-tort lawyer, a better personal-injury lawyer, or, for that matter, a better human being—here's the only tarnish-free rule I can give you: Be utterly and completely sincere when you say the words, "How can I help you?"

Because there's real power embedded in those words if there's sincerity attached to them.

If I've learned anything over the years—as the head of a firm that has brokered hundreds of millions of dollars in settlements for our clients—it's that every client desires some variation of the same response when they seek legal counsel.

The thoughts running through most people's minds go something like this:

Listen to me.

Listen to what I have to say.

Listen to my story.

Show me a lawyer who's constantly burdened by "client-control problems," and I'll show you someone who's neglected to take the time needed to actually listen intently to their clients' needs.

I know plenty of lawyers who can construct legal arguments so dizzyingly clever they could impress the United States Supreme Court. But here in our corner of the legal industry, within the fields of personal injury and mass torts, empathy and razor-sharp business instincts are the real differentiators.

If you're the kind of lawyer who's always in a hurry—speeding through depositions, adding your opinions to every conversation, and pushing your own timeline and agenda—you're never going to live up to your true potential.

You can hone and spit shine your client pitches all you like, but if you lack the common sense—not to mention the human decency—to treat every single soul who walks into your office the way you'd hope to be treated, you're doing an injustice to yourself, your firm, and your profession.

My advice? Personalize and internalize your clients' every wound and fear. Address all of their questions and concerns. Be transparent about who you are, what you plan to do, and how you'll work within the confines of the system to help redress their wrongs.

In short, be unabashedly sincere when you ask the question, "How can I help you?"

If you can do that, I can teach you the rest. I can teach you how to grow your firm. I can teach you how to acquire more clients and how to hire and empower people who ensure you enjoy long-term business success.

But none of those practical skills matter if you don't possess the drive to actually help change other people's lives.

I'm not sure if empathy can be fully taught. But there's no doubt that it has to be actualized from the inside. You have to flip that switch yourself. No one else can activate it but you. So consider this book to be a story of how I found my own unique definition of purpose. It's a book focused less on legal strategies and more on the interpersonal and business strategies that so few lawyers ever talk about in public.

Most of all, it's a book about change—a look at how my personal background as well as my firm's work on a landmark sexual assault mass tort involving the University of Southern California changed my clients, our firm, and me.

I hope in some small way that our efforts helped change society at large as well. And by recounting moments from my life as well as key events from the University of Southern California (USC) case, I might help you change too—both personally and professionally.

Let me be clear about one thing: I'm proud of my firm and my profession. But I am extraordinarily wary of attorneys who cast themselves as all-powerful messianic figures. Hopefully, when you close the back flap of this book, I'll have provided you an honest survey of my life—revealing both my warts and beauty marks—as well as the inner workings of a successful mass-tort law firm.

Change, as I think this book will show, requires collaboration. It occurs when, and only when, a diverse cross-section of people marshals the courage to reject the status quo.

Change is a by-product of individual and collective traumas and triumphs, our professional setbacks and career advances. It's born out of legal victories as well as a practical understanding of how money can be wisely and effectively deployed.

By no means is this book meant to be an exhaustive moment-by-moment account of the USC sexual assault case. It's better to think of it as a series of discrete revelations, which sways back and forth between the past and present, between personal principles and practical business advice, between meaningful moments from my own life as well as key turning points in our case.

SUCCESS IS NOTHING MORE THAN THE OPPORTUNITY TO LEARN SOMETHING NEW AND VALUABLE FOLLOWED BY A DESIRE TO USE THAT KNOWLEDGE TO HELP SOMEONE ELSE ACHIEVE THE SAME.

When I was younger, I used to think successful lawyers, by definition, were people who earned vast sums of money and basked in the exalted glory of prestige and celebrity. In recent years, I've simplified my definition of success a great deal. At this point in my life, success is nothing more than the opportunity to learn something new and valuable followed by a desire to use that knowledge to help someone else achieve the same.

This book is a collection of ideas and pearls of wisdom that I've collected over the course of my life. Do with these teachings what you may. Hopefully, my experiences will help you avoid some of the pitfalls that I made and hasten your journey toward wherever it is you wish to go.

Nevertheless, it is a call to action. I hope it serves as a rallying cry for all of us, within the legal industry and outside of it, to leave our profession and our communities a little better than the way we found them.

Maybe you want to make more money. Maybe you want to help strengthen an existing movement. Maybe you want to reconnect with that powerful sense of purpose that motivated you to want to become a lawyer in the first place, many, many years ago.

Defining that professional purpose is entirely up to you, but I do know that handling mass-tort cases has dramatically altered the trajectory of my life. And I'm writing this book to prove that there's absolutely nothing preventing you from finding similar success. But the process invariably begins by asking your clients a very simple question: "How can I help you?"

And meaning every single syllable when you say it.

CHAPTER 1

ANSWERING THE CALL

ARE YOU REALLY LISTENING?

"I think I was sexually assaulted." Those were the words the young woman confessed to me—very quietly, very nervously—over the phone one afternoon in 2018.

Note her choice of words. The inherent trepidation in that sentence. The fear of being judged. "I *think* I was sexually assaulted."

Let's dispense, right from the beginning, with the saccharine cliché of the wounded survivor in need of help and the heroic knight-errant lawyer who swoops in to save the day.

At the time, there's no way I could have known that this single phone call—from a woman we'll refer to as Betty, for the sake of anonymity—would set off a chain of events that would culminate in the single-largest sex abuse settlement in the history of American higher education.[1]

Change, as I've learned, doesn't arise from a single act nor occur in a glorious, sweeping upward motion. It whittles its way toward progress in furious fits and starts.

It's not caused by one person—or one decision. It's the product of a great, big messy collage of small yet important ideas that somehow fuse together to form a dramatically greater and far more powerful whole.

For if the #MeToo movement has taught us anything, isn't it that we should listen more and dismiss less? I'd argue that same principle applies to becoming a better contingency-fee lawyer as well.

Anyone eager to play a prominent role in a real movement, much like our crusade to bring sexual assault survivors out of the shadows, can benefit from becoming a better listener.

The best way to start? Apply both a literal and metaphorical interpretation to the phrase "answer the call."

We've been conditioned to hear the phrase "answer the call" and view it as someone stepping forward to accept a daunting challenge. But don't forget about its more plainspoken meaning.

Sometimes "answering the call" simply means picking up your phone and listening to the voice on the other end of the line. Because that's how every case, large and small, inevitably begins.

For mass-tort lawyers like myself, these cases always begin with a stranger and a story—followed by willingness to carefully listen to a potential client's trauma.

Betty's call marked the first time my firm had ever taken on a mass-tort sexual abuse case. We'd worked on other torts, including major cases involving BP, Roundup, and Yaz birth-control pills, as

---

1   Matt Hamilton and Harriet Ryan, "USC to Pay $1.1 Billion to Settle Decades of Sex Abuse Claims against Gynecologist," *Los Angeles Times*, March 25, 2021, https://www.latimes.com/california/story/2021-03-25/usc-payout-gynecologist-sex-abuse-claims-to-top-1-billion.

well as a wide array of personal-injury cases. However, if I'm being honest, taking on a headline-grabbing sexual abuse case was uncharted territory for us at the time.

The most gut-wrenching moment—the stomach-churning nadir—in any case tends to come early on. For me, it's the moment when a stranger builds up the courage to reveal, in nervous fits and starts, just how dark this world can be.

This is why I encourage all of my lawyers to focus on becoming better listeners.

Listening doesn't mean seizing every break in a conversation to show how smart you are or how successful you've been in years past. Listening isn't about you; it's about understanding the unique needs of the person who's coming to you for help.

Forget about what *you* want to say. What is your client saying to you? Sometimes it's not about money or potential settlements at all. Often enough, survivors just want you to lend an ear and listen as they describe the horrors they've experienced. They want someone to look them in the eyes and say, "I'm sorry. That was wrong. What you went through should not have happened to you or anyone else."

That is, in my opinion, the first and very simple step in becoming an instrument of true change.

My clients have shown me that there is a great deal of bravery to be found in this world if you know where to look for it. And they've also taught me that there's true evil lurking in the shadows, especially if you shut your eyes to what's happening outside of your own private bubble.

FORGET ABOUT WHAT *YOU* WANT TO SAY. WHAT IS YOUR CLIENT SAYING TO YOU?

As my conversation with Betty continued, she described the kind of black-hole evil that can swallow people whole.

Here's what I heard that afternoon. It's the facts as I know them, which I hope captures some of the pain and bravery of our first USC client.

Prior to our call, Betty had obtained my phone number from a friend, whom I'd previously helped with a personal-injury case. Initially, Betty was reticent to open up to me, revealing only small fragments of her story, piece by careful piece.

Nevertheless, I could tell, right from the start, that she was a smart and articulate young woman, who'd obviously been carrying around a great deal of deep-seated pain for some time.

There's an art to conducting introductory calls like these. Young lawyers often ask me how they can build trust with a total stranger. How, they ask, do you forge a connection with a disembodied voice on the other end of a cell phone?

My simple advice? Never ask questions in a way that might be misinterpreted as an interrogation. The last thing you want to do is shatter the confidence of someone who has had to tape, tack, and glue together their confidence just to call you.

Sincerity and gentility, that's what you're looking to convey. And, of course, patience. Never rush it. Always allow the survivor to unspool their story at their own pace.

Don't judge; just listen. You can scrutinize, if need be, the details of their story later. What you really need to do is deploy some good old-fashioned empathy. Make a connection. It doesn't matter if it's a classic slip-and-fall case or a $100 million mass tort. Building trust should always come first.

Gradually, Betty let her guard down and offered more details about her life. She'd been born into a rough neighborhood in the Midwest, the kind of place where good grades don't carry much value. But to Betty's credit, those pressures never deterred her from being an all-star student. She worked hard to realize her potential and did well enough in high school to receive a scholarship to USC.

For Betty, that scholarship felt like a golden ticket, a one-way flight to a different world. If there was a drawback, it was that she'd have to leave the only place she'd ever called home.

Betty was proud that she would be the first member of her family to attend college. Some people in her circle showed genuine excitement; others harbored thinly veiled jealousy. So as the weeks went by, internal doubts began to surface. She began to feel nervous about her upcoming move—the kind of trepidation that I, too, experienced as a young boy moving from London to the United States.

Uncertainty. Alienation. Isolation. Those were the primary emotions Betty told me she'd experienced on the plane ride going west. Upon arriving in California, she felt an immediate need to connect with something—or someone—as quickly as possible.

One evening, she met a young man. She saw something in him, perhaps something that reminded her of home. Feelings developed. Looks were exchanged. And in time, she chose to sleep with him.

Given the circumstances, it wasn't a very unusual decision. College life, for many women, is marked by new relationships. But when Betty recounted this part of her story, she slowed down, as if she was driving over a dangerous speed bump. Caution reemerged in her voice, knowing full well that this was the one part of her story that had the ability to elicit unfair judgments.

Maybe sleeping with the young man was a mistake, she told me. She wasn't sure. But she was absolutely sure about what happened next. Betty made an appointment to see a gynecologist, Dr. George Tyndall, on campus to ensure she wasn't pregnant. Tyndall was the sort of physician most people viewed as being beyond reproach. He was a well-known pillar of both the medical community and the greater USC campus itself.

This is when Betty arrived at the real crux of her story—the point where her voice began to crack.

Betty is, as I'll later see firsthand, a tall, smart, attractive young woman. Dr. Tyndall, she tells me, noticed her beauty right away.

Initially, there was a chaperone in the room, but at some point, the doctor ordered that individual to leave under the pretense that he needed to examine his patient alone. Betty was asked to take her clothes off. She thought nothing of it and followed her doctor's orders.

She had assumed, as any young woman might, that she'd come to a safe place, a well-lit treatment room affiliated with USC.

"What was I going to do," I remember Betty asking me over the phone, "other than do what he asked me to do?"

That's when it began. Betty was sitting naked in a pair of stirrups. Dr. Tyndall was asking her questions that confused her. He kept insisting she describe her most recent sexual experience. Warily, she recounted the encounter.

This is when the doctor said something that made her cringe. "You have," he said, "a very attractive vagina."

What's a woman—any woman, regardless of her age—to do, sitting naked in a chair, when a doctor says something so skin-crawlingly licentious? Betty decided to just keep talking, to nervously brush it aside as if it was an awkward joke. But as I hope we've all come to realize, ignoring abuse or an abuser's advances rarely makes the problem go away.

Betty's doctor, sensing he'd overstepped his bounds, quickly returned to his previous line of medical questions. He wanted to know if there had been a history of disease in her family. Or if she felt sick or uncomfortable in any way. She answered, "No."

And then Dr. Tyndall asked her a second question, which made her stomach curdle even more. Betty's doctor asked her if she had reached orgasm during intercourse with her partner.

She paused for a moment—stunned—but ventured forward with an honest answer. "No," she told her doctor; she had not reached orgasm. Betty's response seemed to please the doctor. He managed to say, in the most professional tone he could muster, that it was quite possible she had a medical problem that he could help her fix.

Maybe she couldn't reach orgasm, he posited, because there was something wrong with *her*. Perhaps there was something wrong with *her body*.

So Betty continued to sit there, still naked in the chair, as he removed a latex glove from one of his hands and proceeded to give her an orgasm manually.

Afterward, he rose up from the stirrups, right at her eye level, smiled, and said, "There you go. There's nothing wrong with you. Turns out, you're OK after all, Betty."

The silence of another awkward pause filled the room. Betty told me that she felt a mix of confusion and revulsion wash over her. Her new doctor quickly filled the silence. "Just remember," he told Betty, "to make another appointment before you go, so I can make sure everything is still OK the next time I see you."

It was while recounting this vile exchange that the older and wiser version of Betty paused and asked me the most soul-crushing question of the day: "Mr. Miller, is there anything I can do?"

Occasionally, people will ask me when and why I chose to become a mass-tort lawyer. And the most honest answer I can give them is usually the least satisfying one: I didn't experience a single epiphany. Nor did one life-altering moment set me down the path that I ultimately chose.

It was a culmination of small moments, both struggles and triumphs. The reason why I do what I do—and why I'm dedicated to encouraging others to join me in what I feel is a noble fight—lies partially buried in the pain and triumph of my own history.

Where I come from—and what I've seen—is one of the reasons why I felt compelled to dig deeper into Betty's story and shine a light on the dark labyrinth of sexual abuse that has gone unchecked for far too long in so many universities across the country.

Perhaps in telling these twin stories—my story and the story of Betty's sexual assault—others might feel emboldened to actualize their own potential and demand justice from those who have wronged them. Perhaps someone reading these stories will see aspects of their own histories in some part of Betty's own journey and summon the courage to fight back against their oppressors and find equity and justice under the law.

In the past, I used to open most of my talks by telling stories about the work my firm did in connection with the BP oil spill in 2010. Or the series of pelvic mesh cases that I helped settle in 2019. But now, whenever I give a speech about mass torts, I talk about my experience representing women like Betty and the extraordinary case that followed.

After ending my initial call with Betty, I remember placing my phone on my desk and slowly reclining into the back of my chair. Moments of complete and deafening silence are relatively rare in my line of work, but if there was ever a moment I needed to cocoon in silence, this was it.

What do you do—where does your mind drift—after someone shares something so deeply painful and personal?

I remember folding my arms tightly against my chest and feeling slightly defensive. And very, very angry.

Given all the clients I've represented over the years, you'd assume that this young woman's story would've been less shocking to me. One would assume I'd developed enough calluses, around both my brain and heart, to dull the impact of her story.

Only that's not what happened at all.

My first thought went immediately to my daughters. I have four children, two of whom are smart and ambitious young women. Not long before Betty's call, my oldest daughter had told me, in no uncertain terms, that she planned to go to college in California—on scholarship no less—to become a doctor.

I couldn't help but wonder, as a lawyer and a father, what was really going on behind the scenes at some of our country's most prestigious universities? I kept thinking about how vulnerable young female students must feel when they leave home and step foot for the first time on a college campus. What assumptions had I made—had *most* of us made—about contemporary college life, campus safety, and the gatekeepers who are paid to ensure a safe educational environment?

"Perhaps," I thought to myself, "we've been fed a dangerous fairy tale." And that the far grimmer reality remained buried somewhere below the surface, just waiting for a group of dogged true believers to come along and unearth it.

A string of questions flitted through my mind. If, God forbid, something like that happened to my daughter or one of my daughter's friends, would they know what to do? Would they know how to react, both during the assault and in the wake of it?

Would they try, over time, to bury the memory of their trauma? Would they keep silent? Or worse yet, would they feel compelled to blame themselves—to ask the wrong questions, like "Was I too nice to him?" or "Maybe this was my fault." Would they try to rationalize an unequivocally evil act?

As I sat there, volleying dark thoughts toward the sunlight beyond my window, I felt a responsibility to answer that call. How many other "Bettys," I wondered, had been abused by this same doctor? Who was going to find those women and document their stories?

And, in a much broader sense, who was going to shine a light on the malignant systems that allowed—or perhaps even encouraged—these assaults to take place?

But what really angered me—what made my stomach do summersaults—was the fact that I'd been partially ignorant as well.

After all, I'd heard the term "sexual abuse" countless times before. I understood, in an abstract sense, the issues involved and the pain it could elicit, but I'd failed to understand the depth and breadth of the PTSD (posttraumatic stress disorder) that followed.

The abuse perpetrated against Betty may have occurred more than a decade ago, but the pain of that experience had become branded into her. She told her story with all the clarity of someone who'd experienced it mere hours ago. The memory of the assault had attached to her like a parasite, sucking life and confidence from her body and her future. Would Betty ever, I wondered, be able to fully shake free from the lingering effects of that assault?

I realized, in that moment, that there is a permanence to sexual assault that I'd underestimated.

For me, this is how it always starts. In every serious mass-tort case I've ever been involved in, they always start—if I'm to be perfectly honest—from a place of discomfort. They start in a state of pure, unadulterated incredulity.

I say the same kinds of things every single time: *How did this happen?* How *could* this have happened? And how can this *still* be happening?

Make no doubt about it. There are potential clients who call up lawyers hoping to try to get something for nothing. They will craft elaborate stories in the hopes of financial gain. They'll lie to seek fame and attention. They'll stretch the truth at the mere prospect of a stranger validating their story.

But I could tell, after my initial conversation with Betty, that there was something genuine in her story, something that demanded further investigation.

Over time—with additional research, further education, and subsequent conversations with survivors—an open-minded lawyer might be able to shed some of his initial naivety about the subject. But that would, of course, take time and effort.

I knew this much. If you want to be a mass-tort lawyer, the question to ask yourself always comes down to this: What are you going to do with a closely guarded secret, once you've been let in on that secret?

What was I—Darren Miller—going to do to prevent subsequent abuse and corruption from harming the next Betty?

Power, as the old adage goes, corrupts. And absolute power corrupts absolutely. But it also corrupts unevenly, slicing swiftly, like a scythe through fragile wheat, across our most vulnerable communities.

We all, to some degree, go through life with blinders on, myself included. *Where we come from. What we do for a living. Where we live.* Our individual experiences distort our ability to see what lies beyond our own experiences.

Yet if there's a blessing to being a mass-tort lawyer, it's that we occasionally cross paths with people who force us to peer, however briefly, into the dark, dank places we'd never seek out voluntarily.

That was the initial gift Betty gave me that sunny afternoon in 2018. She gave me a reason to start reeducating myself. She penned the first cryptic page of what would become a far more complex mystery.

Our conversation sparked so many questions. Chief among them was simply this: What exactly was happening behind closed doors within the medical systems of our universities?

Timing may not be everything in life, but it's a key supporting player. I'd like to think I would have been just as tenacious in pursuing this case fifteen years ago as I was today, but I can't be sure about that. The truth is people gravitate to the mass-tort industry for all sorts of reasons. It would be disingenuous for me to say that the prospect of large settlements—good, old-fashioned money—isn't the primary motivating factor for some people.

Everybody wants to make more money. It doesn't matter if it's the janitor down the street or the CEO of a global Fortune 500 company. I want to make money. You want to make money. But if you're successful over an extended period of time, as I've been, you start to change and shift into a new gear.

Evoking real and lasting change suddenly becomes just as important. This might sound trite on paper, but it's exponentially more satisfying to make money while you're simultaneously helping to make the world a better place.

IT'S EXPONENTIALLY MORE SATISFYING TO MAKE MONEY WHILE YOU'RE SIMULTANEOUSLY HELPING TO MAKE THE WORLD A BETTER PLACE.

Those were the thoughts ping-ponging through my mind as I rose from my chair, called my team into my office, and told them it was time to start taking a deeper look into Betty's story.

I needed to know more. There was no time to waste. I was heading in one direction, down from my cozy barrister's existence into the subterranean world of collegiate sexual abuse. Time to start digging. But I needed help. I needed my team to crawl down into the darkness with me to try to unearth some light for Betty and countless other survivors like her.

CHAPTER 2

MAKE IT PERSONAL

USE YOUR HISTORY TO SHAPE YOUR FUTURE

I don't care what new technology comes hurtling our way in the years to come. There's no substitute, anywhere in this world, for face-to-face interaction. At some point you have to make it personal. Lawyer meets client. In the flesh. Eye to eye. Voice to voice. Physical presence meets physical presence.

I'm no Luddite. You won't find a more ardent proponent for the adoption of bleeding-edge technologies in the mass-tort field than yours truly. I invest and leverage technology and artificial intelligence and proselytize to lawyers, with all the enraptured passion of a born-again preacher, about the need to stay a hundred leagues ahead of the technological curve.

That said, there comes a time in the life cycle of any case when you need to wind back the clock and go old school. No more phone calls. No more text messages. No more video chats. Just you and your client sitting in a room, sizing each other up.

It should become pretty clear to you when that moment has arrived. You'll have completed your initial round of research and begun shedding some of your initial doubts. That smoldering fire in the pit of your stomach will start raging like an incinerator. That tiny jolt of static electricity you felt during your initial call will intensify until it feels like a live wire spitting out electrical charges.

Paradoxically, you'll find this feeling usually flares to life when it's also become abundantly clear that the odds against you and your client winning have dipped so low that Vegas wouldn't touch them with a plus $10,000 money line.

That's the day worth circling on your calendar.

That's the moment when you have to toss aside every time-saving technological crutch you can think of, get up from your chair, and go meet your client in person. That's the only way to truly know if you're ready to play David to some deep-pocketed Goliath. It's the only way to find something in yourself—something buried in your *own* personal history, some established pillar of your *own* belief system— that overlaps with the client sitting across from you.

In the case of Betty and her sexual abuse charges, that moment arrived after my team and I began researching other allegations leveled against the university.

If you want to be a good mass-tort lawyer, you have to be willing to play amateur investigative reporter somewhere along the line. You need to go looking for every scrap of supportive evidence you can find. You need to be willing to spend weeks—if not months—combing through the internet. And you need to be able to analyze and scrutinize those documents to build a strong case.

In doing our own due diligence, I was surprised to find how many other complaints had been cautiously typed, texted, and uploaded by students who'd been under the care of Dr. Tyndall. Granted, each seemed to be slightly different, but when pieced together they generated a suspicious matrix of activity.

There were plenty of bread crumbs to follow. Many of the accounts followed a similar pattern: Someone visits Dr. Tyndall's practice at USC. Some suspicious or uncomfortable event occurs behind closed doors. The survivor complains to a friend or administrator. And then nothing happens. There's a curious silence, as if no one will deign to acknowledge the possibility of abuse, let alone attempt to address it.

Our research sent my radar pinging. Either, by some miracle, all of these young women from around the world had gathered together to concoct the same exact story, or we were staring at systemic negligence, not to mention decades of cover-ups, within the University of Southern California.

But this supposition raised other questions: What was the university really hiding here? That's the question I wanted answered. What couldn't we see, as outsiders, trying to peer into the darkened windows of the ivory tower?

My mind kept drifting back to the chaperones who were supposed to stay in the room with Dr. Tyndall's patients. Was there some sort of signal from Dr. Tyndall that let them know that they should leave the room? And if so, why didn't these chaperones immediately report this suspicious activity to the university? Was it out of fear of losing their jobs? Were they complicit in this action? Or were they completely unaware as to what was happening when they were signaled to leave the room?

Within a month of my first call with Betty, I called her back three to four more times. After each conversation, my initial instincts about the veracity of her story only grew stronger. She not only was strikingly consistent in how she described the abuse, but she also began to divulge other details that others might never have had the courage to admit. In addition, she was frank and convincing in how she described the psychological toll of the abuse.

She told me how she eventually dropped out of school and flew back to her hometown in the Midwest. How she struggled to make ends meet, while she processed what had happened and why. As well as the ebb and flow of psychological paralysis she felt in the days and months thereafter.

I couldn't help but listen to her story and feel as if my own life—my own family's unique journey—had been surreptitiously leading me to this very moment. Escaping the crushing cycle of multigenerational poverty isn't easy. Even if you're one of those fortunate few who finds a way to scrape and claw your way out, you still carry the weight of that journey—and its resulting scars—with you wherever you go.

You can't understand the toll that an attempted escape from poverty can have on your body and psyche by observing it through a TV screen or reading about it in a book. No movie or news story will ever truly do it justice.

Simply put, there are those who've lived it. Those who know they are just one wrong step from sliding back into the abyss. And those who've merely gazed at it from a distance, ignorant of its true wrath, protected by their financial security.

My parents flat-out lived it, enduring their own set of difficulties in the Caribbean.

As a young boy, they used to tell me stories of their early struggles and how profoundly that journey shaped their lives. Both were born into large families—my father in Jamaica, my mother on the island of Nevis, a sister city to Saint Kitts—but neither grew up with the benefit of an intact nuclear family. My dad lost his father at a young age, and my mother never knew her father, a fisherman who went out onto the water one day, suffered a terrible accident, and never came home.

When my sister and I were children, my mother used to tell us vivid stories of her upbringing. It's no exaggeration to say that my mother was dirt poor. I use that term in a literal sense, meaning she lived in the dirt in a small one-room shack, divided into two quadrants by nothing more than a single flapping sheet stretched from one wall to another.

She didn't have the luxury of indoor plumbing. If my mom—or any of her seven siblings—needed to use the bathroom, they'd have to use a nearby outhouse, which was nothing more than a hole dug into the ground. If they wanted to take a bath, they trudged their bare feet along a jagged and dusty trail, a couple hundred yards away, to a stream where they could clean themselves or wash their clothes.

There was never enough food in my mother's house, but there were always platoons of filthy rats. I remember her describing the queasy sensation of small teeth gnawing at her exposed toes in the middle of the night.

Only it wasn't a nightmare; it was her reality.

She'd curl up and then, almost as if it was a learned reflex, strike back with forceful kicks. That was the equally nauseating part—the feeling of her hardened feet kicking against dirty splotches of rat fur and gnashing jagged little teeth. The sensation of those teeth chewing away at her has never left her to this day.

Try as she did to paper over those haunting memories, her eyes used to peer out into the distance when she spoke of her youth, bending time the way an X-ray passes through skin seeking the solidity of bone. My mother could always see through people—and see beyond tragedies—the way few others could.

As a young boy, I listened intently to these stories, but I'm not sure I truly understood them until I was thirteen years old. At the time, my mother had scrounged up just enough money to send my sister and me back to Nevis to meet my grandmother and my aunt Florence.

My parents saved up for years for us to take that trip. It must have meant a lot to my mother to send us back to her home. Looking back, it was an important moment in my development, which helped me understand my parents far more clearly.

After enduring their hardscrabble upbringings, my parents met in London. Both had decided to place a big bet on higher education. My mother worked as a nurse. Meanwhile, my father pushed himself to earn a degree—taking night school classes, no less—in electrical engineering. They were both extremely hard workers. Somehow they found a way to push through the significant segregation and class discrimination that they encountered in London—where I was born and lived until I was ten years old—in part because their strengths complemented each other's talents so perfectly.

My dad was a dreamer, warmly social and uproariously gregarious. What surprised a lot of people, I think, was that he was a great listener too. My mom was practical, caring, and trustworthy. She was the grounded one, who worked long hours as a nurse plus second jobs to put food on the table, while my dad pursued his dreams and further education.

While we were in New York, she'd come home in the morning and fix us a little breakfast before shipping us off to my aunt's house, where we'd stay until we left for school. That was the only short stretch of time when she could sleep before she headed out to her next job.

When I became a teenager, I think my mother felt it was important that my sister and I see, with our own eyes, where she came from.

When we arrived in Nevis, it was just as she had explained it, only now it loomed before me in startlingly drab three-dimensionality.

I could see it. Touch it. Smell it. Feel it. A single-room shack, no bigger than a one-bedroom apartment in the United States. It was plopped down, remote and isolated, in a desolate pasture. Here, spread before me, was the small plot of land where my family had lived for thirty or forty years. Only they didn't own it; they rented it. It wasn't theirs; it always belonged to someone else.

The reality of life outside our little bubble stared back at me with cruel, uncaring eyes for the first time in my life. I'd finally seen what was hiding beyond the curtain—nothing romantic or bucolic, just that same flimsy sheet flapping in the squalor and the wind.

Looking back, that trip couldn't have occurred at a more significant time, in terms of my own mindset and maturity. When you're thirteen years old, you haven't quite crossed the threshold into full-fledged adolescence, when you can force yourself to ignore the reality laid before you. Yet you're old enough to absorb—and catalog—the raw emotions that bloom inside of you.

I remember my grandmother running around, preparing a meal for my sister and me. She made it sound like she was preparing a feast, but when we sat down at her table, all she could slide onto the center of her table was a malodorous piece of fish surrounded by rice and a swarm of hungry flies. In that moment, I know we looked unappreciative, despite the fact that there was more food on that meager table than my grandmother ate in a typical week.

It was sparsely seasoned and, to our Americanized palates, tasted downright insipid. My sister turned to me and whispered, "I can't eat that. There's no way I'm eating that." But I'd begun, in that moment, to finally understand the stories my mother had shared with us.

It wasn't an abstraction anymore. I'd finally seen everything with my own eyes. No amount of imagination would ever paint our family's history in bright Caribbean watercolors. It would forever remain, in my mind's eye, sheathed in dark, sad hues—buzzing with flies.

In retrospect, it was an invaluable gift. During that dinner, I realized why my parents had sacrificed so much to move us from the precipice of poverty into a kind of bridge state, where the fortunes of my sister and I could either rise higher or slide back into the hole from whence they came.

And in one of those rare moments when a thirteen-year-old kid does the right thing instead of the easy thing, I whispered to my sister, "We are going to eat this food for Mom and Grandma." On the one hand, it was an unpleasant experience, but on the other, it was redemptive. For it taught me the importance of leaving my gilded perch, journeying out into the world beyond my comfort zone, and meeting people and tragedy head-on—eye to eye, face to face, person to person.

I carried this lesson with me into my legal career. When I first began handling mass-tort cases, I read about a series of plants and refineries in Port Arthur that were spewing poisonous gases into nearby communities. Despite evidence of the dangers these toxins presented, very few lawyers—or reporters, for that matter—took the time to visit the minority victims who were breathing in these noxious fumes.

Their concerns were not only ignored; the corporations running those plants were always sidestepping the sword of justice. Occasionally, they'd pay nominal fines—less painful than even the proverbial slap on the corporate wrist—and slow down for a stretch before they'd start poisoning their neighbors all over again.

At some point, I determined that I couldn't keep myself at a distance any longer. I had to go down there—down to Port Arthur—and see their living conditions for myself.

I remember parking my car, getting out, and gazing up at these huge scalloped billows of smoke tunneling their way skyward. It looked like I was watching the aftereffects of the Challenger shuttle explosion, snaked coils barreling into the sky and then falling toward the earth like a filthy blanket. So I walked across the neighborhood and started knocking on doors and talking to people. They all told me some variation of the same story.

At some point, they'd point up at the sky, toward the putrid man-made fog descending over them, and say, "Shouldn't we be able to breathe in our own neighborhood?"

Where could these people go? Most days, they couldn't escape their own living rooms. And they certainly didn't have enough money to abandon their homes and flee what had been, to my mind, a crime scene. They were stuck there, as if someone had poured wet concrete on the ground, knowing it would harden around their ankles.

These were conditions I wouldn't wish on my worst enemy. But they were their reality—their *normalcy*. An inescapable fact of life.

That experience reminded me of my parents, who used to constantly remind me of a rather difficult truth. "There was nothing flawed," they used to tell me, "about poor people who failed to find a way out of poverty. They didn't lack intelligence or grit."

And thus I was constantly reminded never to fall prey to the illusion that my family was better or more special than our old neighbors who didn't flee.

The word my parents preferred to use was "fortunate." They felt fortunate to be able to find themselves in the United States. And with this good fortune, my sister and I had a responsibility to make things better for other people. It's one of the reasons why my parents always sent money back home when they had a little extra cash to spare. And why I work in the particular field I do, the legal arena, to this day.

I was allowed to make many mistakes when I was younger, except the cardinal sin of looking down at anyone. "You don't know their circumstances," my mother and father would tell me. You don't know where they came from. You don't know what opportunities were given to them, which rugs might have been pulled out from under their feet through no fault of their own. Their parental instructions always receded back to one central golden tenet: don't assume anything of anyone until you learn the truth of someone's story—their *whole* story.

This invariably brought me back to thinking about Betty. She'd somehow been pushed back into the deep, dark hole she was trying to crawl out of. She'd been born into poverty. She seemed to be on her way to making it out, climbing out of the darkness into the sunshine. But then she was kicked back into that hole, only this time she wasn't alone down there. There was someone else waiting there. A doctor who shooed away chaperones and closed the door to his office, effectively trapping her inside. And when she reported these actions, the university did nothing more than heap extra dirt atop that hole until she couldn't see the sunshine anymore.

After each of our calls, I could tell there was more to her story than she was ready to reveal. Something was preventing her from recounting her whole story. I realized I needed to offer her something more than an open ear.

She wanted to meet me every bit as much as I needed to meet her, so I did what all lawyers should do when they find themselves in a similar situation. I decided to meet her on her own turf.

I asked Betty if she would be comfortable allowing me and one of my female team members to fly up to Illinois and talk to her in a location of her choosing.

She paused and then said, with an undercurrent of relief, that she felt that would be all right.

I knew immediately who should join me: Marcela Jackson.

I needed a fighter but also someone who was inherently empathetic. That can be a difficult mix of character traits to find, but Marcela and I have gone into battle by each other's side so many times over the last eighteen years that I knew she was the woman for the job. Simply put, she's a fabulous asset to our firm. And everyone in our line of work needs to find their own Marcela to enjoy true long-term success.

Marcela embodies all the traits I wanted for this particular visit with Betty. I wanted someone who was simultaneously fiery and nonjudgmental. Intelligent yet showed an ability to forge instant bonds. If I had to leave Betty and Marcela alone for any reason, I knew in my bones that they'd be able to converse honestly and openly with each other—woman to woman—no matter what details Betty chose to share.

What I needed was a self-made woman. Everything that Marcela has earned has been of her own making, born from her own tenacity and hard work. The fact that she managed to achieve all that she has while basically raising three wonderful children on her own makes her accomplishments that much more impressive.

This led us to the big day. I'd purposely let Betty decide where we would meet because I wanted her to feel as comfortable as possible. She chose a local bar not too far from where she lived. It was neither big nor particularly trendy—the sort of place where every regular seems to know each other's names.

Needless to say, Marcela and I arrived there early. It's almost sad that I have to stress this to young lawyers, but you never, ever want to be late for a meeting, let alone an initial in-person exchange.

It's always helpful to observe a client as they interact with their surroundings. Are they gregarious and open? Or shy and nervous? If you can glean some clues as to their personality, you can tailor your approach accordingly.

In Betty's case, Marcela and I chose to sit at a table way in the back of the bar, in an elevated little nook by the restrooms. I always look for a seat in the back of a room, which offers clients some semblance of privacy.

We watched the doors open and close until I spotted a young, attractive African American woman stroll around the room, as if she was casing the place. She looked at me but then quickly pivoted away, assuming I wasn't the lawyer type.

I felt, instinctively, that this woman was Betty. But since I couldn't be 100 percent sure, I called her cell phone to see if she'd pick up. As soon as she did, I walked over to her and introduced myself.

She was, in a word, shocked. I don't think, for whatever reason, she thought I was a Black man. Nevertheless, she seemed relieved. It proved to be an unforeseen icebreaker, a welcome surprise that instantly put her at ease.

The truth is I get this kind of shocked reaction quite often. It's unfortunate how binary the world can feel for African American lawyers. I've learned that I have to be somewhat bilingual when I speak to others. If I'm talking with my boys, I'm expected to adopt an entirely different verbal style than when I talk with clients, which often demands a more professional patois.

In this case, that versatility proved invaluable because Betty felt she could speak naturally, in a way that might have been off-putting to some stuffy, middle-aged white lawyers. She could express herself in a way that came most natural to her. And as she began to talk, some of the missing pieces of her story began locking into place.

We talked for ninety minutes straight—not a single awkward or uncomfortable break among them. It just flowed—talking, smiling, and laughing. I've always felt that you need to be genuine—to build a runway—before you delve into the more sensitive issues. Most lawyers break that golden rule with shocking regularity. They rush headfirst into questions about the tort or adopt an almost paternalistic approach.

In sensitive cases like this one, you'll know it's time to start talking about the case when—and only when—your client broaches the subject.

> **I'VE ALWAYS FELT THAT YOU NEED TO BE GENUINE—TO BUILD A RUNWAY—BEFORE YOU DELVE INTO THE MORE SENSITIVE ISSUES.**

Before we ever set foot in that bar, I told Marcela we might end up spending the whole night in that bar without mentioning the case. You can't be in a rush in instances like this. I was prepared to close the bar and head right back there tomorrow, if I had to.

Your client should always dictate the speed and flow of the conversation during an initial meeting. In this case, Betty was comfortable enough to eventually broach the issue of her abuse at USC, which is when she dropped the bombshell. Turns out that the abuse she initially described didn't occur once or twice. It occurred over a two-year time period. Her doctor had set up multiple appointments and assaulted her in a multitude of ways for two straight years.

The details came pouring out of her, only some of which I feel comfortable sharing in this book. Dr. Tyndall kept circling back, time and again, to that cringe-inducing line: "You have a beautiful vagina." He'd ask her if it was OK if he photographed her vagina, leaning back on the fake concern that there may be something wrong with her body. He'd take pictures from different angles. He'd tell her that he needed to look at her vagina more closely, to the point where she could feel his breath inside of her. And during some visits, Betty told me that he masturbated in her presence.

It was enough to make anyone's skin crawl. At the same time, I knew it changed the nature of the case dramatically. This *was* systemic abuse. And the frequency and manner of the abuse raised all sorts of questions as to how a doctor could get away with this kind of behavior for such an extended period of time.

There was one nagging question, however, that I felt I now had a responsibility to ask. I needed to know why Betty kept going back. Why did she keep returning to the clinic, appointment after appointment, to see this man?

Her answer came down to youth and experience. She was just a teenager, she told me. She was a young woman living on a university campus in California. Her doctor was telling her there could be something wrong with her reproductive system. He was her gynecologist, the head of the department. He was telling her that everything he was doing was necessary. She had no idea what standard protocol was. She was worried, so she kept telling herself, "Who am I to tell this man what to do during an examination?"

In short, he was the predator, and she was the prey. I thought back to my mother and all those rodents nibbling at her toes. This man—this so-called doctor—was nothing more than a modern-day manifestation of those filthy Caribbean rats. And Betty's attempt to reach out to me was her attempt to kick back.

So I made a pledge to Betty, right then and there. I told her my plan of action. I told her that I not only believed her, but also I promised to suit up and fight for her with every ounce of my being.

I told her that I knew too many people who'd attempted to rise up, only to be pushed back down into the pit. And that she should rest assured that I was going to stand up to anyone—the doctor, administrators, the entire academic community if need be—who attempted to silence her.

I'd file as many complaints as I needed. I'd fly out to California, just as I flew up to the Midwest, to fight for her. My goal was not only to get her restitution for her abuse but also to do everything I could to level the playing field for the next Betty who found herself in a similar situation.

I told her I couldn't guarantee that we'd win because neither the world nor the system always works the way they should, but I wanted her to know that she had a fighter in her corner. And to recognize that I wouldn't stop swinging until the last bell rang. I promised Betty that I'd never curl up or sell out like all the other people who could have stepped up and helped her in the past but chose not to. And that she would indeed get her day of justice.

The decision to accept or reject any offer from USC was going to be *her* decision. We'd take this case all the way to a jury if she wanted to. I wanted her to feel, despite the horrors she'd experienced, that the power was back under her control.

I told her that I wanted to carry this fight forward, not only for her but for all the other women who might find themselves in a similar situation days, months, or years down the road.

That's when the tears started streaming down her face. She'd wipe one salvo away, and the next would quickly replace it. I could tell that our paths had crossed for a reason. To which she said, "Thank you, Mr. Miller. Thanks for choosing a side."

CHAPTER 3

KEEPING THE FAITH

A MASS-TORT PRIMER

Dream big dreams. That was always my father's advice to me, both in word and action. He taught me, more than anyone else in my life, that setting lofty aspirations is *an* essential prerequisite for finding success in life.

Personal and career growth always starts on the *inside*. It's about faith, vision, and hard work. Lucky are the few who stumble— horseshoe in hand, four-leaf clover pinned to their lapel—into a fairy tale of self-actualization and professional achievement.

For the rest of us, success is a by-product of belief and hard work. But there's no question about the order of operations. A steadfast belief in the promise of a better future has to come first.

Say it with me: "Faith."

Faith is the kindling that sparks action. Faith in yourself. Faith—despite all the warts and temporary injustices—in your chosen profession. And faith, above all, that you are capable

FAITH IS THE KINDLING THAT SPARKS ACTION.

of transubstantiating your dreams into realities.

It's so important for everyone involved with a mass-tort case not to lose faith. One of our jobs, as lawyers and entrepreneurs, is to find ways to motivate people, to give them a reason to keep fighting—to keep pushing the battle forward. If you're angry that someone pulled you over for no reason. If you're angry at the system, whether it's the entire structure or a particular judge or politician, it's OK to lose one battle. But to win the war, you need to find a way to have faith in yourself.

As an African American lawyer working in Texas, I've experienced more than my fair share of discrimination. Sometimes, you can sense it right away, before anyone even utters a word. Especially in boardrooms and conference rooms. It kind of hangs in the air like an odious cloud. Anger won't dispel it. You have to fumigate it yourself.

You can see it, subliminally on people's faces, in flitting eyes and sweaty palms. Who is this big Black guy entering our space? It used to bother me but not as much these days, because I've learned that part of my responsibility now is to educate people. I'm a teacher as much as a lawyer.

If someone prejudges you, the best thing that you can do is to go about your business and prove their biases wrong. Debunk their prejudices with thought and action. I show the people who I am, what my skill sets and abilities are. And in doing so, I force them to recognize they're judging me incorrectly.

The same principle applies to being a mass-tort lawyer. You want to drop jaws and wow people? Then use your wisdom as a weapon.

Show everyone in the room that you understand their business or their cases better than they do.

I do it all the time. And it's a sweet feeling when you feel that cloud lift. And all of a sudden, people will start extending their hands for you to shake them. Next thing you know, someone is inviting you to come meet their family, their wife, their children. You gain acceptance on your terms, not theirs.

And here's the sweetener: you've changed them without changing yourself. You've left a boardroom and a group of people a little more enlightened than you found them. That's the payoff. When the next lawyer walks into their orbit, they are going to have to deal with less bullshit than you did.

For a great number of lawyers, a belief in mass torts tends to take shape as they grow older. It's a story as old as time. Successful personal-injury lawyers tend to view their work as a vocation. It truly is a calling. We are drawn to the challenge of trying to restore feelings of safety and joy that were stolen from our clients. We are driven to find a modicum of justice by holding those responsible for that pain accountable for their actions.

Only my origin story—my desire to practice a particular kind of law—goes back much further, back to London, England, in the late 1970s.

Picture this scene. It's 1979. I'm a curious kid, lounging around in a small living room, flipping through the channels. Mom is working. Dad is studying. My sister is off doing something else. And I've just finished my homework.

What are my options? I've got BBC 1. BBC 2. BBC 3. BBC Who Cares.

My eyes are glazing over like fresh-baked donuts.

Basically, I have a menu of two options: homegrown British programming, dry as a three-day-old scone, or a slurry snowstorm of hissing static. Given I'd inherited my father's imagination, there were relatively few TV shows that captured my attention.

Back then, I craved American TV shows. Give me the American dream, however mythical Hollywood was choosing to depict it. Give me heroes and heroines. Give me drama. I wanted to read books and watch shows where the stakes were really high. Adrenaline. Speed. Excitement. I wanted to consume narratives that were unmoored from the British class system and social mores that enveloped me in school. Stories that could portal me to distant places filled with lovable and oddball characters.

I'm flipping. Stuffy Edwardian dramas? No thanks. *Flip*. Corny Monty Python shtick? I'll pass. *Flip*. And then, magically, there it was—an American TV import by the name of *Petrocelli*.

Truth be told, I probably couldn't stomach watching a full episode today. Young Darren, however, was absolutely transfixed by the images unspooling before his eyes.

There it was, in all its grainy late-70s glory—a show about an American lawyer, who seemed to be sprinting through each day at an Olympic pace. Now *here*, young Darren mused, was a life worth dreaming about. Fast cars. Breakneck action. Clandestine client meetings shrouded in mystery and danger. Courtroom dramas. It had it all.

I appreciated the fact that the main character really cared about the various strangers who walked into his office. I liked that he was part lawyer and part teacher, dispensing sound advice about the law and life in seemingly equal measures. Not to mention that he used the law like a cudgel to right societal wrongs.

It's funny the things that stick with you. I remember being mesmerized by the way the main character carried around his briefcase. That leather satchel of his felt downright otherworldly. When he opened it, pulling out bundles of game-changing evidence, that briefcase felt downright magical.

I remember whispering to myself, "I want to be *that* guy someday. I want to be the kind of lawyer who has the power to thwart evil and change people's lives for the better."

Looking back, it was probably pure Hollywood hokum; nevertheless, it inspired me. It gave me something to dream about—an aspiration to run toward.

For ten-year-old Darren, becoming a lawyer checked all the right boxes. These were smart men and women who were respected and upwardly mobile, yet the fictionalized lawyers in my favorite show were guided by a higher purpose. They

BELIEF FUELS ACTION.

seemed committed, as cliché as it may sound, to using the rule of law to improve the lives of the downtrodden.

I remember my teacher going around the classroom one day, asking each of us what we wanted to be when we grew up. I think 90 percent of the boys in my class aspired to be soccer players. I said that I wanted to be a lawyer. Not a British barrister. An American lawyer. And I held firmly to my answer despite the ripple of giggles that burbled up around me.

From that moment on, I didn't just say I wanted to be a lawyer. I told people I was going to *become* a lawyer. If I've learned this much in life, it's that there's a wide delta between wanting something and becoming it.

My point is simply this: belief fuels action.

To me, a life dedicated to the legal field felt like predestination. There was no doubt in my mind that, one day, I'd be living my own version of the events I soaked up from that blurry old TV screen.

I mention this story because faith is something good lawyers must share with their clients. It's the cornerstone of any long-term attorney-client relationship.

At some point clients like Betty have to muster up the courage to believe in two things. First and foremost, they have to believe in themselves—to recognize that they're survivors who possess enough grit and resilience to see a case to its logical conclusion. And second, for a mass-tort claimant to be successful, they must find a way to believe in the promise of the mass-tort process itself.

That's where we, as their lawyers, need to educate them on the benefits of initiating a mass tort as opposed to taking other legal actions.

If a group of survivors has been abused in a similar fashion by the same perpetrator, they can collectively pursue a civil action. Although class actions are uncommon in most sexual abuse cases, it was an option in the USC case, albeit not the best course of action available.

I meant everything I said to Betty when we first met in her hometown. Ultimately, she had the final say in regard to many critical decisions, especially when it came to deciding when to settle and how much to settle for.

That being said, there is one critical early decision—the first junction in a complex matrix of choices—that is a take-it-or-leave-it proposition at our firm. When it comes to sexual abuse cases (or pretty much any group lawsuit for that matter), I firmly believe that the advantages of joining a mass-tort lawsuit invariably outweigh pursuing a class action suit.

Here's why. Those working outside our space often confuse mass-tort actions and class actions, which are two fundamentally different legal actions.

Let's begin by breaking down some basic terms. In the legal world, the word "tort" is used to describe any wrongful action that has been performed by a given party. This wrongful action can be committed by anyone—a corporation, an academic institution, a government, or a medical system.

In all of these cases, a defendant is being accused of contributing in some way, whether intentionally or unknowingly, to harming or injuring another party.

If we start with a definition of a tort as our foundation, simply adding the word "mass" allows us to see that a mass tort arises when a group of people who've suffered similar injuries inflicted by the same party comes together to file a joint lawsuit.

As the old saw says, there is strength in numbers. No corporation or academic institution is going to quake in fear over a few isolated lawsuits, but if numerous survivors band together, they stand a much greater chance of forcing the defendant to address their injuries and negligence.

As to be expected, the court system welcomes these group lawsuits, as it doesn't possess the bandwidth to handle hundreds—if not thousands—of individual lawsuits against a single defendant.

It all comes down to efficiencies. Group lawsuits prevent the court-clogging bottlenecks that would occur across the country if each case had to be tried individually. They also prevent defendants from being forced to litigate each case separately, which lead to a never-ending legal merry-go-round of litigation and courtroom appearances.

To ensure all of these cases are handled in a timely and efficient manner, the court allows some plaintiffs to consolidate their individual lawsuits and pursue justice against a single defendant. If they choose to file a collective lawsuit, they join other plaintiffs who've been injured in a similar fashion by a common defendant. Often when lawsuits are filed in this fashion, the courts decide to organize these cases into something we call multidistrict litigation.

Mass torts and class actions differ in how each individual plaintiff within the group is viewed by the court. In a mass tort, each individual claimant is treated as an individual, who just happens to be a member of a larger group.

Take, for instance, the famous mass tort involving asbestos products that began in the 1970s. When the defendants were found guilty of negligence in that tort, certain silos of injuries and rewards were established. Claimants who developed, say, late-stage cancer were awarded larger settlements than those who developed injuries like chronic obstructive pulmonary disease.

When it comes to a class action, every claimant is lumped together into what we call a class, and individual members of the group, called class representatives, are often chosen to stand in for the group. Whatever judgment is ultimately rendered applies to everyone in the class, whereas in mass torts, each situation and injury can yield a different award.

We don't participate in class action cases at our firm, primarily because individual clients rarely receive the financial resolutions that are commensurate to the injuries they've experienced.

This is due to the way class action lawsuits are structured. In a class action case, a judge appoints a lawyer to spearhead the class action suit, which means that individual lawyer can receive a disproportionate amount of the attorney's fees.

Personally, I don't like class action lawsuits. I've seen too many instances where clients walk away with nothing more than a pittance, while their attorneys earn hundreds of thousands or even millions of dollars in fees. In every one of the mass-tort cases I've been a part of over the last twenty-plus years, mass-tort clients always walked away with a greater share of the money than those who opted for a class action.

I can't say for sure this will always be the case, but here's what I do know for certain: in the mass-tort sexual abuse case I've recently settled, there were thousands of class action survivors who received less than $3,000 in settlements. My mass-tort clients, by contrast, will often receive average settlements of seven figures each, despite the fact they suffered similar injuries.

This being said, I know there are reasons why some sexual abuse survivors opt to pursue class actions as opposed to mass torts, most of which come down to just two general factors: speed and anonymity.

I understand now, in ways that I failed to previously, the PTSD that lingers in one's psyche—and body—long after sexual abuse has occurred. I've spoken to women who can't bear the thought of reliving their abuse, as it requires unearthing old memories and answering questions during a deposition.

I respect their desire to insulate themselves from future trauma, and I understand why they feel more comfortable passing the baton of representation off to someone else.

That being said, I've also spoken to women who've made it clear to me, in no uncertain terms, that they wanted to pursue a mass tort, only to go home and have their husbands talk them out of it.

These are absolutely soul-crushing decisions to witness because it gives us all a window into the pressures that can emerge at home, behind closed doors, or when spouses apply pressure to their partners to stay silent.

I've heard a wide array of nauseating justifications and counterarguments as to why abuse survivors shouldn't participate in mass torts: *The abuse happened so long ago; why can't we just move on from it and leave it in our past? You don't want the risk of your families finding out or media attention.* Or the classic excuse, *What if someone countersues us, and we lose everything we have?*

Logic, in many cases, fails to trump the specter of fear. It doesn't matter that we can virtually guarantee anonymity. That we can enter our clients into a mass tort as a Jane Doe or that we can shield them from inappropriate questions during depositions. Nor in some cases does it matter that mass-tort clients have the option of dropping out of the suit at any time, should they become overwhelmed.

For some families—and some individual survivors—the threat of unearthing old traumas is simply too much to bear.

In the end, I firmly believe that the great differentiator between choosing to pursue a mass tort versus a class action comes down to faith. Does the client in question believe in their chosen lawyer as well as the mass-tort process itself?

Do they believe that their lawyers have their best interests in mind? Have they seen enough, both in word and action, to believe they have a champion in their corner who's going to fight for them?

Amassing that burden of proof doesn't lie with the plaintiff. That burden lies with us, as their lawyers. I can point to piles of statistics that show women who chose class actions as opposed to mass torts have left millions of dollars on the table.

In most cases, that's enough to encourage some abuse survivors to allow us to do what we do best, which is to force corporations, academic institutions, and other negligent actors to pay for the trauma they've inflicted on others.

In some ways, I think I'm at my best when I can channel my inner ten-year-old, the young Darren sitting in front of the old TV set, dreaming about doing good. I'm at my best because there's something deeply rewarding in fighting for individual clients—knowing every face, listening to every story—so they can find their own justice.

It's the difference, in short, between lawyers you *hope* to trust one day and those, deep down inside, you *know* you already trust today.

CHAPTER 4

TEAM BUILDING 101

ONE TEAM, ONE FAMILY

There's no use sugarcoating this. Faith may be the cornerstone of every successful mass-tort campaign ever waged. *Faith in your own abilities. Faith in your client's story. Faith in the mass-tort process itself.* But belief devoid of a carefully honed presuit strategy will derail even the strongest of cases before they ever hit a courtroom.

I can't underscore this point enough, especially for young mass-tort lawyers. Most cases are won or lost early in the process, long before you file a single document. Obviously, winning successful verdicts is impossible without the support and efforts of skilled litigators, but if you want to build an enduring mass-tort *practice,* it all comes down to process, process, process.

Think of it like a recipe. In the early going, you have three primary responsibilities:

Step 1: Assemble the best team possible.

Step 2: Do your research.

Step 3: Devise a battle plan.

That first component—team building—can be deceptively difficult. I can't tell you how many lawyers have approached me over the years, wanting to know how we've built a team that works so efficiently and cooperatively.

My vetting process can be distilled down to five golden rules.

Rule number 1: You can't teach grit. Show me an intelligent, hard-charging self-starter, and I'll show you someone who's going to exceed even your loftiest of expectations.

Rule number 2: Empathy is a superpower. If you stare across a table and see a skilled applicant or lawyer who's capable of showing a client the same amount of care and attention as you do, hire them and never look back.

Rule number 3: Find people who can see around corners. As cases progress, you'll need a coalition of advocates who can anticipate every potential trap, trip wire, and tire spike that might be tossed onto your path.

Rule number 4: Recruit people who are aligned with your firm's internal culture rather than those who happened to earn a degree from a prestigious college. In most cases, passion and desire burn much brighter than an Ivy League pedigree.

Rule number 5: Second-chance hires tend to be great hires. Never be afraid to give someone who might have temporarily lost their way a second chance, because they'll often fight like hell for you and your clients.

If you're going to go to war, you better have an ironclad battle plan in place before you even think about throwing the first legal punch. And to formulate that plan, you can't rely solely on your own instincts. You need to rely on the collective wisdom of everyone inside your firm.

Sounds simple enough, right? Building a strong team is a completely obvious first step. Oh, but it's a slippery one—pure black ice— for a shocking number of law firms.

Here's why. To wage a successful mass-tort campaign, you have to humble yourself, ditch your ego, and lean into the collective wisdom of your team rather than merely follow your own instincts.

IF YOU'RE GOING TO GO TO WAR, YOU BETTER HAVE AN IRONCLAD BATTLE PLAN IN PLACE BEFORE YOU EVEN THINK ABOUT THROWING THE FIRST LEGAL PUNCH.

Everybody in your firm knows what you think, but do you know what everyone around you thinks? Furthermore, have you ever stopped to ask them?

No one's omniscient. Do you think, at this point in your life, you can possibly see the world the same way that someone making fifteen dollars an hour does? Or someone who's stuck in a dead-end job living in a dead-end apartment in a dead-end neighborhood?

Educate yourself, but also be open to being educated. And then go out and, if possible, return the favor by educating the world at large. That's the order of operations that generates true change.

I am, for instance, a self-avowed news glutton. When I'm not working, I'm reading and watching the news. Magazines. Newspapers. Websites. Facebook. TV and cable news. Twitter feeds. YouTube. It's a smorgasbord—a never-ending buffet of news feeds and media content.

I crave diversity. Local news. Domestic news. International news. Give me as many different stories from as many different sources, perspectives, and parts of the country as possible. Feed me what I don't yet know, and I'll be better because of that new knowledge.

As far as some of my friends are concerned, my insatiable hunger to absorb the news is so all-consuming they'd probably stage an intervention if they could. When, for instance, we go to a poker room, and I see ten TVs all streaming sports, I'll ask someone to flip one to CNN. I watch sports as much as any other guy at my table, but I also watch the news. I'll gladly watch both, but I want options. I want different perspectives. I want different content.

Sometimes, when I've folded a bad hand, I'll scan the room to see if anyone else is paying any attention to that one lone TV broadcasting the news. Most nights, everyone's eyes are glued everywhere but that screen. It will be completely and willfully ignored by everyone in the room.

I say, "Don't follow the crowd. Resist the temptation to keep your eyes glued to your own screen and your own reality." Too many lawyers are too concerned with what they already know and not enough about what others can teach them.

If you find yourself researching a subject or area of the law that is outside your area of expertise—as we did when taking on USC— don't be intimidated by what you don't know. Ignorance isn't always a handicap. In some cases, it can be an extraordinary asset if you allow people to teach you things you don't yet know.

If I'm to be perfectly honest, it took me a while to understand this.

Case in point, in years past, I developed a bad habit of running meetings like I was a college professor lecturing to a group of bored undergrads. It was *The Darren Miller Show*. Same time. Same channel. Every single week. That dais was mine. I never relinquished the floor.

My job was to talk—and everyone else's job was to listen. So many lawyers make that mistake today; they want to hear themselves talk instead of taking the time to listen to those around them. Listening is how you learn; you don't learn or grow by droning out everyone else with your ideas.

What can I say, other than it was a temporary lapse in common sense? And I learned my lesson. Leading is not spoon-feeding. It's creating a space for open dialogue.

In years past, I'd call internal meetings and relay everything I'd learned to my team. There was no give-and-take. I told people what I *thought* they needed to know.

I gave a lot and asked for little in return, which I now recognize was a mistake.

Because when I was finished for the day, I'd scan the room and see the same exact thing: nodding heads and empty smiles. The teacher had spoken. The lessons, I assumed, had been absorbed. My job was done here.

Not so.

In time, I realized I'd fallen into the same bear trap that ensnares so many of the lawyers I'd vowed never, ever, to emulate in my own practice. You reach a certain degree of success in this profession, and you start to believe that *you* always know best. Maybe you've heard that voice in the back of your head whisper things like, *I'm the one who built this firm into what it is. I'm the one who's bringing in all the really big cases. That's my name on our letterhead—and my name on the front door—so everyone better just shut up and follow my orders.*

Over time, logic slapped me upside the head. I said to myself, "Hey, hold on a minute here, Darren. Why are you trying to do this alone? You can't read everything. You can't watch every newscast. Read every Facebook post and Twitter feed. Common sense told me that more than a hundred people pulling together could achieve a lot more than one man working alone.

My plea to you is simply this: democratize your process. Treat your people like family, and they will give you more than you can imagine.

I made the sort of small changes that any lawyer reading this book can do tomorrow morning. I called a meeting and said, "I'm changing the way we run meetings. We're shifting from the all-mighty 'me' to the more powerful 'we.'"

From then on, everyone was expected to do their own research and share what they found with the group. Every member of our firm, from our lawyers and legal assistants to processing agents, were expected to contribute. I wanted to hear everyone's thoughts.

It didn't take long before I realized how much collective intelligence and curiosity had been hiding in plain sight. Everybody was expected to bring something in—a story, a valuable insight, a finding—and share it. And that simple change helped give people more ownership over their work, which in turn motivated them to work harder for the women we represented in our USC case.

They certainly opened my eyes about just how pervasive sexual abuse is on college campuses today. As I write this, there are studies suggesting that one in five women and one in sixteen men have been abused while in college, with as much as 90 percent of those abuses going unreported.[2]

And the research conducted by my team helped us unearth extraordinary findings about USC. From 2000 to 2014, a former health center director at USC covered up eight complaints about the doctor who abused Betty.[3] And from 2013 to 2014 alone, five students

---

2   Pennsylvania Coalition Against Rape, "About Sexual Violence," retrieved April 1, 2022, https://pcar.org/about-sexual-violence.

3   D. Miller & Associates, "USC and Dr. George Tyndall Sexual Abuse Lawsuit: 'A Walk in Their Shoes,'" August 29, 2018, 1:10–1:40, https://www.youtube.com/watch?v=Tb_o0CG1vnw.

refused to be seen by the same doctor because of negative experiences while under his care.

If there was a flaw in our early system, it was that everyone had too much information to share. And on occasion, some critical ideas would fall through the cracks. Around that time, hernia mesh cases began to really take off. And we'd been late to the party.

I called a meeting and asked, "How did we miss this?"

One of my legal assistants spoke up and said, "Mr. Miller, I told one of our attorneys years ago about those hernia mesh cases. It was important to me because it affected someone in my family, but we never talked about it again, so I just let it go."

That exchange made me realize that we needed to create more of a formalized structure to collect and store our ideas, so we built an internal chat room. We leveraged technology to make it easier for people to share their ideas and knowledge. If someone came across a link about an interesting story, heard something on a newscast, or wanted to share a personal anecdote that they felt was pertinent, they added it to the chat room.

Soon we were upgrading our tech to better organize those findings and tag them for quicker access. And the results were extraordinarily powerful, in terms of expanding the scope of our work.

One of our team members started posting about an absolutely horrifying scandal unfolding in Louisiana, where a local parish was rewarding cops for ticketing African Americans. The theory was that they could dissuade Black people from living in their parish—or even driving through it—if they ticketed them as often as possible.

I would've never known this was happening had our team member not brought it to our attention. At one point, a police officer showed the courage to come forward and say, "This is real and systematic.

This is happening right now, and I can't do this anymore. I can't do this to my own people."

So we went out there and got involved. We hired a local attorney to find survivors and argue that these people's constitutional rights had been violated. These racist policies not only had to stop, but survivors of these crimes needed to be compensated for the crime.

It comes down to this: as my fellow Texans say, "Don't be a cowboy." Lean on the diverse views and skill sets of your fellow team members. You think you have a sound strategy in place? You think you're pursuing the right cases? Good for you. Now prove it by calling a meeting and encouraging your colleagues to pick it apart, piece by piece. Welcome input—and dissent—from *everyone*. And you'll be shocked at just how productive your next series of meetings will be.

When it came to our USC case, I called a lot of meetings in the early going, making sure to alter where and when we met. Some meetings were held at our office, and some were held off-site. The goal, in terms of the latter, was to help break up our routine and encourage people to think outside the box.

Before these meetings, I'd send out an agenda of open-ended questions that I expected them to consider prior to the meeting. I wanted my team to mull over what was at stake in this case—and the impact that this firm could have on these young women's lives as well as the academic establishment as a whole.

I tried, as best I could, to paint a detailed account of the trauma Betty experienced and to underscore the point that Betty was no outlier. I've been a mass-tort lawyer long enough to know that when I see smoke like the kind Betty described, there were bound to be others getting burned by the same fire. I knew there had to be other survivors out there, waiting to tell their story.

It was our job to find them, but when it came to conducting interviews with sexual abuse survivors, I felt we needed a more specially trained abuse counselor to provide our clients with an extra layer of support.

I feel it's extraordinarily important that mass-tort firms constantly adapt and change to meet the needs of each tort. No one wants a cookie-cutter law firm, a one-size-fits-all shop. It's my job—and my team's job—to properly assess which clients we will be representing, the case in question, and the unique set of circumstances that the upcoming battle might bring.

I'd learned this from the work we did on the BP Deepwater Horizon oil spill in 2010. I was surprised to find how many of our clients minimized—instead of exaggerated—the issues and problems they faced in the wake of the spill. I remember, in particular, a fisherman who couldn't make a living due to the damage caused along the shore. His business didn't just suffer; it dried up completely.

Here was a man, through no fault of his own, who suddenly found himself with no source of income. I needed him to tell me how the spill had upended his life. I needed him to tell me what was going on in detail, but he wavered for weeks.

It took time, but eventually he told me how his life had spiraled out of control after the spill. His wife continually badgered him, blaming him for the family's inability to make enough money, until she had an affair out of spite and left him. She said she needed someone who was more of a "man" than he was, someone who wouldn't be crippled by a rogue thunderstorm.

Alone and unable to pay his rent, he was forced to move in with his brother. For the longest time, my client didn't want to talk about any of this. Didn't want to give us any of the salient information that we needed for the case. He was embarrassed. He saw himself as less of a man for expressing grief and pain. From that moment on, I vowed to always—and I do mean always—surround myself with people who are adept at forging connections with the clients we represent.

I want teammates who never judge. People who can lift our clients up emotionally while we work through the courts to get them justice under the law.

In getting to know Betty, I realized we needed to offer her and our sexual abuse survivors full-time support. We not only needed to represent them but help them overcome the pain of their abuse in every way we could.

This pressing need, which I expressed to my team during our meetings, was a by-product of what they'd taught me about the lingering trauma of sexual abuse. I realize now how deep and enduring the psychological wounds of abuse can be.

I've talked to women who've shown me how a single instance of traumatic abuse can irrevocably wreck people's lives. No more parties. No more dating. No more talking to men in social settings. Many women seek out ways to insulate themselves from the pain of their abuse. Some survivors never fully recapture their previous identities; others wrestle with thoughts of suicide.

As mass-tort lawyers, we have to be honest with ourselves. We can't do it all. None of us can. But I will always remain steadfastly committed to helping survivors find some semblance of "normalcy"—however they choose to define that term. And to do that, I knew I had to recruit someone our clients could open up to on an entirely different level than they could with me. Someone who'd survived their own sexual trauma and dedicated their lives to helping others do the same.

This much I've come to learn: far too many lawyers feel they can be saviors—that they are the sole and all-mighty conduit of hope, healing, and empowerment for their clients. I've come to the opposite conclusion: if I can stand back, outside of the spotlight, and hire someone equipped to generate hope and healing, sometimes that can be enough.

I'll gladly take the back seat, knowing that one life empowered from afar can catalyze a thousand others to come forward. For it's in these small victories—finding counselors who can encourage others to speak the truth—that true change is possible.

But I also realized we needed to add another lawyer to our team. I felt that some of our clients were going to feel more comfortable speaking to a female attorney, no matter how well intentioned my fellow male lawyers and I might be.

This wasn't a token hire. I didn't want to hire a female lawyer simply because she was a woman. We wanted a lawyer who'd displayed some legal muscle—a prosecutor with an established track record of putting dangerous abusers behind bars. Someone who could stand before a judge, jury, and opposing counsel and describe how she'd helped the courts punish these predators in the past.

I asked my team to help me scour every nook and cranny to find worthy candidates for these new positions. So we talked, as a group, about what type of qualities we wanted to see in these candidates. Not just in terms of education but in terms of personality and process. I might have offered up an initial template, but in the end we came to a consensus as to what we needed as a firm.

I'm a big believer, as I've already noted, in establishing and voicing lofty goals. A clearly defined purpose is, without question, a powerful motivator.

A CLEARLY DEFINED PURPOSE IS, WITHOUT QUESTION, A POWERFUL MOTIVATOR.

I made it clear to my team, as soon as I heard Betty's story, that I wanted us to cocreate one of the most trustworthy sexual abuse mass-tort law firms in the country. And to do that, we needed to defy convention and ensure our firm looked—and acted—differently than other firms.

How would we do that? By recruiting special people. And I do mean special. Everyone I'd called to that meeting already possessed unique talents, perspectives, and knowledge. Ultimately, they would have to help me find more people just like them.

It's imperative, in my opinion, to hire people who align with your firm's value and culture. Want to hire a seasoned specialist who will cost you $500,000 a year? Go for it, but if they're going to want to do things their way instead of the way your team does them, you're going to struggle in the long run. Square peg meets round hole.

It's better, I found, to start by asking basic questions: What is their level of commitment to the case in question? What additional tools or help does the candidate need to be successful? Has the candidate fostered a reputation for being selfless and passionate about causes larger than themselves? And above all, are they teachable?

You want to be a successful mass-tort lawyer? Then think like an entrepreneur. There's a story from my own childhood that I've shared with my own children when they were younger. It's not a particularly epic story, but it's one of those early life lessons that I've carried with me my entire life.

When I was a boy, my mother struck a deal with me. If I made my bed and mowed the lawn without her saying a single word, she'd give me five dollars every week. Knowing a good deal when I heard one, I immediately started making my bed and cutting the lawn, which netted me my weekly Abraham Lincoln.

I'd spend my dollar on gum, then go to school—where I'd earned the title of the "Candyman"—and sell every piece of gum for twenty-five cents each. Suddenly, my small bundle of cash multiplied, leaving me with plenty of extra money to buy more candy and do with my profits what I pleased.

There happened to be one kid in my class, Keith Bahry, who had an insatiable sweet tooth. He was perpetually asking me for free candy, to the point that I gave him "candy advances." Over time, we became friendly and began hanging out, and it became clear to me that he was a savant when it came to mowing people's lawns.

I hated mowing our lawn. And I was never very good at it either. So I struck a deal with Keith. If he mowed my lawn, we'd be square, and I'd make sure he was stocked up with enough candy to make his dentist rich beyond imagination.

It was a match made in Kentucky bluegrass heaven. Keith cut our lawn with shocking precision. And I paid for his lawn services with nuggets from my candy stash. What's always stuck with me, however, was my dad's reaction to seeing Keith's work. After Keith's first pass, my dad surveyed the lawn—cut like the infield grass at Wrigley Field—and said, "Darren, how the hell did you get our front lawn to look that good?"

To which I responded honestly, "I have my ways, Dad. I have my ways."

Decades later, I still have my own way of doing things—my own way of planning, hiring, and analyzing legal problems. I have a set of commandments I live by.

Listen intently. Find purpose. Build the best team possible. Hire people who get things done and then lean on them to do what they do best for the benefit of the firm and your clients.

Let me add one more bullet point to the list: I don't believe in micromanaging. I do tell people exactly what I want, but I pride myself on letting them do their jobs, once they understand the way we work and our culture.

Needless to say, many of the counselor candidates our team found were impressive, but I immediately knew whom to hire. There was a young woman named Kim Case, who'd seen and experienced an extraordinary amount of evil in her life. (I will leave out the brutal details of her kidnapping and rape.) But whenever she sits down with survivors, they open up to her in ways that still stun me. What I saw in her, right from the jump, was an incredible ability to listen intently and help others deal with their respective traumas.

Kim wants to help women. She always goes the extra mile to connect survivors with additional services that can help them find balance. When a client buckles, she's there, phone in hand, ready to lift them up.

Her work has shown all of us how difficult it is for some survivors to recount their abuse. Many women block out memories and seal them away in places where we, as lawyers, can't get to them. I know sexual abuse survivors who've delayed interviews or canceled them at the very last minute, even though we, as mass-tort lawyers, need to record those stories for the good of the tort. Kim has taught us all how to give our clients the time and space they need to open up and release their pain.

In regard to finding our prosecutor, I knew I had the right lawyer when I met Rochelle Guiton, a former felony chief prosecutor from Montgomery County. She specialized in prosecuting child exploitation and human trafficking and put away a number of criminals who deserve to be behind bars. She's provided us with extraordinary insights into the psychology of sexual predators. She's the kind of lawyer who's never been afraid to visit the scene of a crime and kick down doors, metaphorically speaking, in order to find evidence that turns strong cases into airtight ones.

I had a host of reasons to make those hires, but there was one declaration I felt needed to be made during our early meeting. An upstart Texas law firm versus a prestigious university teeming with political clout and teams of high-priced lawyers? The odds were not going to be in our favor.

I wanted to make that ultraclear. That's just my style. At times, I need to be unvarnished and completely honest. This was going to be a David versus Goliath kind of struggle. They'd try to bury us. Outspend us. Drag things out until we'd fold.

Our clients were out of state and out of statute. So if we wanted to attain justice, we were going to have to do so as a team.

The only solace I could offer my people was the fact that the country—and society in general—was changing. And it was our job to help quicken that change. My reason for hope was simple. If you found out, as a parent, that you were sending your daughter to a university where her friends were being victimized, would you maintain the status quo? Would you let the school where your daughter was studying get away with that level of wonton negligence?

My gut feeling, then as now, is that no right-minded person would allow these horrors to continue—especially if some brave team showed the courage to bring the truth to light. That, in short, was our singular goal, no matter how long the odds: find more clients. Bring the truth to light and use it to slay a hulking Goliath waiting patiently in its ivory tower in California.

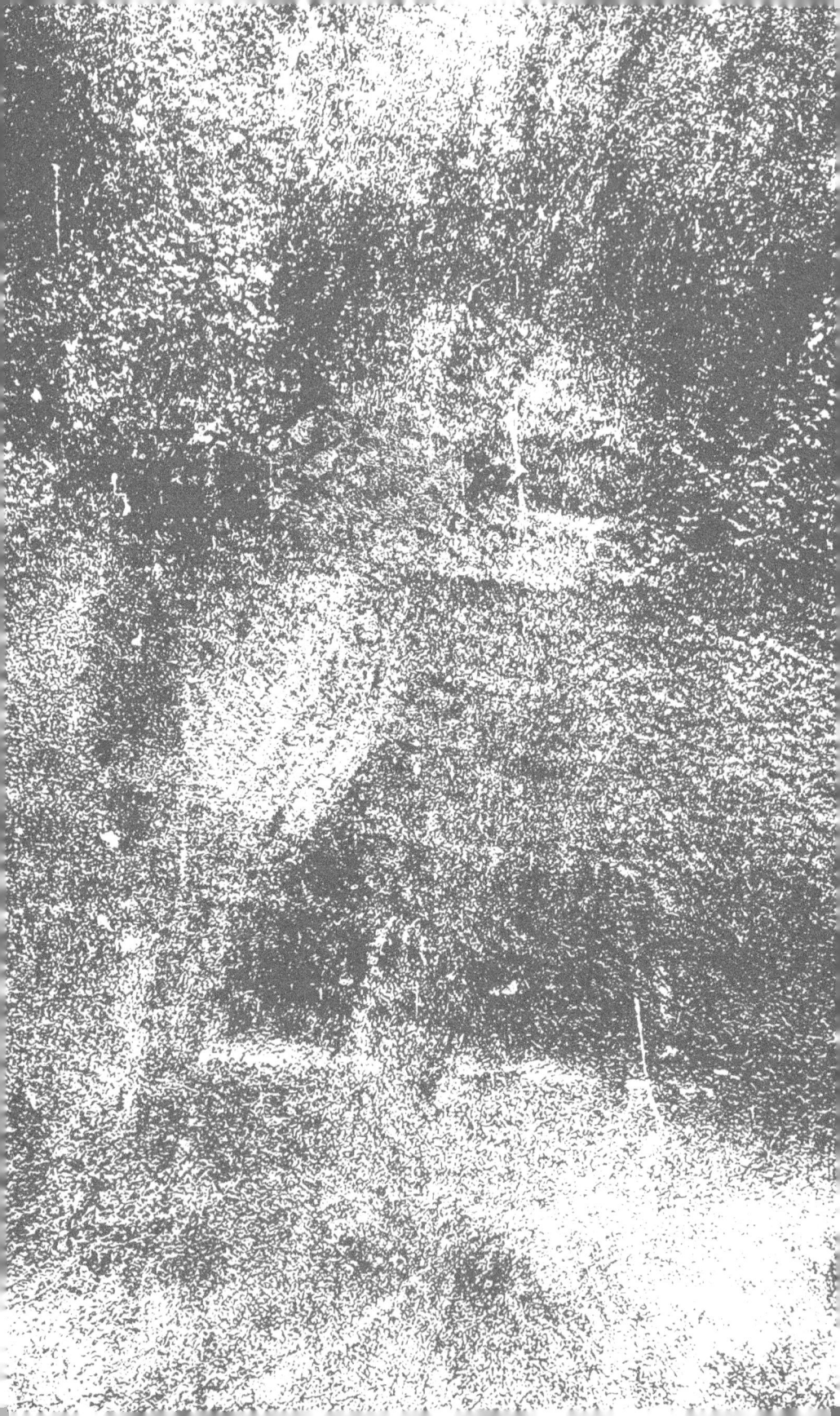

CHAPTER 5

BE THE OUTLIER

WHEN IN DOUBT, GO YOUR OWN WAY

I loathe the word "mediocrity." To this day, even typing it makes me squirm a little. The concept of *failure*? I can't stomach that. If you ever see a lawyer look someone dead in the eye and say they've never lost a case, you can assume one of two things: they are fresh out of law school or are unrepentant liars.

If you're a contingency-fee attorney, you'll lose cases. A client will lie to you. Someone will withhold critical information. A judge, for unexplained reasons, will side with the defense. A jury will see things a different way. You will lose cases.

Disappointment? You should be able to handle that too. Some things, by the law of averages, are not going to work out the way you expect them to. A judgment will pay peanuts when it should have yielded a bonanza. You miss the boat on a massive tort you should have pursued. Just get over it. Tell yourself the second time's always going to be the charm.

Everyone knows a legal lemming when they see one. They are the attorneys who move in packs. The lawyers who lick their fingers to test which way the wind is blowing and then immediately march in step down the same well-worn path that everyone has already trampled through.

I suppose that suits some people just fine. But not me. This much I know about the mass-tort world: it's not for cowards.

If you're not willing to bet on a worthy underdog—odds be damned—you're in the wrong profession. And I'd argue you're probably reading the wrong book.

IF YOU'RE NOT WILLING TO BET ON A WORTHY UNDERDOG—ODDS BE DAMNED—YOU'RE IN THE WRONG PROFESSION.

There's no doubt that my disdain for mediocrity is derived, in some way, from a lecture my father gave me when I was in high school. As an engineer, my father possessed a unique talent for delivering compact life lessons that were so irrefutably logical—*if* A *equals* B, *then, Darren, you're sure as hell going to do* C—that no one could rebut them.

I say that as a compliment. I love my father. To this day, if I need advice or a sounding board, I call my dad. But darn if some of his early life lessons didn't sear themselves so deep into my subconscious that you'd swear he used a blowtorch instead of a few carefully chosen sentences.

Here's one of those lessons. One afternoon, he sits me down and says, "Son, let me remind you that you're Black."

Great lead. Fantastic opening argument. What's a teenager to say in response to that? I'm sure I nodded my head and, being a teenager, said something like, "You're right, Dad. Last time I checked, I was still Black."

But at that point, he already had me right where he wanted me, caught in a rhetorical rope-a-dope. Next up? A couple straight jabs of truth: "Not only are you Black," he said, "you're *very* Black. You come from a family that has very dark skin. And that puts you in a different position from most people. So listen to me when I tell you that you can't allow yourself to even entertain the thought of being mediocre. If you settle for mediocrity, you're going to be passed over. *By everyone*. Mediocrity is going to get you left behind, son. It's going to get you left out in the cold."

"Darren," he said, "you're going to have to separate yourself from the crowd—prove to people that you're not only capable of doing great things but deserve opportunities. It's not enough to be as good as the next guy; you have to be better than him. And the way to do that is by proving to everybody that you're *different*."

No standing eight count. *Straight to ten.* Fight's over. To this day, I've never forgotten those words: *be different*.

Hopefully, some teenager who looks like me or comes from a background similar to mine takes this lesson to heart, because it's an invaluable one. Don't flee from the things that make you different. Your trauma. Your pain. Your family. Your neighborhood. Your upbringing. Your language. It doesn't matter what that difference is. The smart play is to use your differences to your advantage. Embrace your outsider status, because if you stand outside the circle of power and peer inside of it, you're going to see things that the insiders will never notice.

This same principle applies to the world of mass torts, especially when you're taking on cases that others are too scared to touch.

There was a time, early in our USC sexual abuse case, when I couldn't convince anyone to join me in our fight.

At this point, my team and I had done our due diligence. We'd done the research. We were building our team. And we'd begun our search to find additional clients.

I knew we were sitting on a powder keg. At that time, we didn't know how many survivors might be out there. We didn't know how USC was going to react. What we did know was that we were pursuing a university with hundreds of millions of dollars at their disposal, not to mention some very powerful alumni who held extraordinary sway over the media.

We needed help. This was all new to us. Up to that point, we'd never been involved in a single high-profile sexual abuse case in the history of our firm. What we really needed, I surmised, was a partner—a marquee law firm with money and muscle.

Shouldn't have been too difficult to find, right? The facts of this case spoke for themselves. Who wouldn't want to answer this particular call? Who wouldn't want to look their children and grandchildren in the eyes and say, "I was part of a coalition that helped bring the truth about collegiate sexual abuse into the light"?

So I decided to call a friend of mine. Let's call him "Attorney Kevin." I cut right to the chase. "Kevin, let's make a stand. Right here and right now. Together. My firm and yours." I laid it all out for him. All the research we'd done. I walked him through our plan and showed him our full set of blueprints.

And his initial response was positive. "Wow, Darren. This has all the makings of a really powerful and groundbreaking case," he said. "Let me talk to some people."

After some time passed, I reached out to give him a nudge. "Kevin, we don't have the luxury of time. We need to hurry. I need to know where your firm stands on this."

In short order, Kevin got back to me with his firm's response. "Hey, Darren, this case sounds interesting, but we don't have a great deal of experience in these kinds of cases either. We don't really know what really happened. And whatever did happen occurred so long ago; we're not sure it will even matter. Plus, we're a Texas law firm. You want us to go to battle against one of the most powerful universities in the country, which also happens to be in California. I'm sorry to say we're going to have to pass on this one."

As I've said, disappointment I can take. But this particular rejection rattled me. It allowed some unwelcome doubts to slip in through the cracks. I remember driving to my sister's house in Travis County, Texas, for the weekend to try and sort things out.

When I'm at home and things take a turn for the worse, I often turn off my cell phone and take a walk to organize my thoughts. My advice to lawyers who find themselves in a difficult spot? Go find a space—your office, a quiet coffee shop, your sister's house, an abandoned broom closet, whatever it might be—where you can just sit and think.

And if that doesn't work, go sit with someone you love. I'm blessed to say I have plenty of options in that department. My wife. My children. My parents. But I think it was fate that sent me to my sister's place that particular weekend.

My sister and her husband, Eric Moore, are two extraordinary people. They're pastors who run an amazing multicultural church called the Summit Worship Center in Austin. It's not a "praise Jesus and send me a check" kind of organization. They're living the Word.

Spend an hour in their church, and I guarantee you even a devout atheist will feel his soul being lifted heavenward. Thank God my sister is a forgiving soul, because I was a hell of a bratty brother to her back in the day. The appropriate word, I think, is "butthead," considering the countless times, as a teenager, I refused to drive her home from school and instead pointed her in the direction of the bus.

That's all, thankfully, water under the bridge now. A trip to my sister's place is a respite from the chaos of my spinning-top of a life. She knows I'm not going to stop working when I go down there, but she gives me my space.

I remember doing a lot of walking and thinking that weekend. And performing a lot of self-analysis too. What did those guys know that I didn't? Was I being foolish? If a group of billionaire lawyers with money to burn was passing on this case, how were we going to make this work?

Should I return to my firm, tail tucked between my legs, and say, "Sorry, guys. We've made a mistake. We're in over our heads. Let's just let it go"?

We've all been there, haven't we? You experience a setback, and you start to question yourself. Your judgment. Your decisions. Your future.

I remember, as I jogged my way around Austin, thinking a lot about my younger years, my father's lecture about being a young Black man and the importance of being different flickered to life, as did memories of my teenage years.

Funny how that happens. You experience a setback, and your mind immediately connects it back to another moment of vulnerability you've never been quite able to shake.

When I was a teenager, my father made it clear to me—on several occasions—that he didn't think I was living up to my full potential. Looking back, he was probably right. But I think part of his disappointment was rooted in the fact that he wanted me to become an engineer, and I was committed to becoming a lawyer.

Following in someone else's footsteps is a lot easier than forging your own path. My dad wanted me to become an engineer, in part, because he'd already figured out how to succeed within that world. It sounded to him like the safer and smarter path.

In the long run, however, safer doesn't always mean better.

Although he might never have said it directly, I know what he was thinking: "Look where I came from and all that I've achieved by taking this path. Follow in my footsteps, son, and I can help you. I can help you avoid some of the issues I had to endure in my own career."

But I'm not sure he realized how much I'd already taken his advice to heart. *Be different*, he said. And I was taking a different path. I never, ever, shied away from or hid from my "otherness." If anything I steered into it and used it to my advantage, beginning when I was an undergraduate in college.

Given that I was in the top quarter of my high school class, I had my pick of Texas universities. Given the choice between going to Texas A&M University and the University of Texas at Austin, I was committed to becoming a Longhorn. When my friends and I visited UT, we were impressed with what we saw: Cool, vibrant campus. Great centralized location in Austin. The UT football team was on the rise. Plus I'd already asked one of my best friends to room with me. As far as I was concerned, it was a done deal.

I drove down to Austin with my friend that summer to get settled and take exams to see which classes I could test out of. We were loving it—every minute of it—which of course was when I received a call from my father. "Darren, how's it going?"

I was excited, and I told him so. There was a new challenge in front of me, but I felt prepared. It was the same kind of nervous excitement I'd feel taking on USC years later. There may have been an uncertain road ahead of me, but I felt more than equipped to handle it.

This is when my father broke the news to me. "Darren, we just received a letter in the mail from Texas A&M, informing us that they want to offer you a larger scholarship. And since your mother and I are helping you with your college tuition, we've decided you should take Texas A&M's offer. So pack up your bags. You're going to A&M."

My reaction? Stoic silence followed by an incredulous "*What?*"

I told my father I didn't want to go to Texas A&M. I told him that I was already settled in and living with my roommate. A decision had been made. I couldn't switch everything now, at the very last moment.

At which point my father said, "Darren, we need you to go to Texas A&M. They're offering you a lot more money. This isn't a punishment. This isn't a setback. Look at it as an opportunity."

Although I certainly put up a little bit more of a fight, in the end I relented. I hung up the phone, packed up my bags, and headed to College Station. And as it turned out, the move proved to be an excellent experience for me because it forced me to establish my own identity. I knew a few people who were going to A&M, but I didn't have the same social safety net I would have had at UT. And that turned out to be a blessing.

At A&M, I learned how to move between different factions on the campus. There wasn't a particularly large number of African American students at A&M at that time. But at some point during my sophomore year, I remember looking into the mirror and remembering what my dad had told me. "Son, you're Black."

And slowly I began to make a conscious effort to go to different parties on campus and build deeper relationships with some of my Black friends. By doing so, I began to learn things about African

American culture that I never really knew previously. And in doing so, I learned more about myself to boot.

Texas A&M was very segregated at the time, but I moved between my cliques of white and Black friends with relative ease. Soon, I was encouraging Black folks to start partying a little bit with my white friends. And some of my white friends stopped being afraid of partying with my Black friends. It was a rewarding period in my life, because I saw people change before my eyes.

If I'm to be honest, some of my white friends liked the idea of having me around as their token Black friend. They didn't mind going to a football game with me or playing late-night Tecmo Bowl tournaments, but when I asked them to come to a party where *they* were going to be the minority, some backed away. And that was OK by me. That told me something about who they were and how they viewed me.

If anything, those social rejections made me stronger. I had a greater sense of who my people were. Black. White. Latino. Asian. I could move between tribes.

Sometimes in life there's freedom to be found in that kind of self-selection. There's no use trying to be everyone's friend. If someone's scared of moving forward—whether it's with a friendship or a mass tort—let it be. The question to ask yourself comes down to this: What do *I* want to do? Who do *I* want to fight for? Where do *I* want to devote my time and energy?

The same can be said about the world of mass torts. We've made great strides in this country in regard to becoming a more integrated society. There's no doubt about that in my mind, especially in terms of how some people are finding common ground and working together toward a common goal. And yet, when you visit some of the most powerful firms in this country, most are still frustratingly traditional.

They have found success by sticking to what they know and exactly what they've done before. They stick to what they're comfortable doing and who they're comfortable working with. To which I would ask, "Are you really capable of serving a broad spectrum of clients?"

Many of these old-school firms are anything but diverse. I walk into boardrooms all the time that are filled almost entirely with sixty- to seventy-year-old white men. You might see a smattering of female partners and a few minority lawyers. But nine times out of ten, when I'm called into one of their meetings, I'm the only African American in the room.

I'm the one who looks different. And when it comes to pursuing risky cases like USC, I'm the one who's thinking differently too. The one who wants to pave a new course. The one who wants to fight for the outsiders, odds be damned.

My point, of course, is that it's a lot harder to make a name for yourself in the mass-tort world by chasing someone else's cases. Better to chase the ones *you* believe in. The ones that allow you to showcase just how different you are. So go out and be the unicorn; be the outlier. Be the person who's unique enough to actually make a difference.

IT'S A LOT HARDER TO MAKE A NAME FOR YOURSELF IN THE MASS-TORT WORLD BY CHASING SOMEONE ELSE'S CASES. BETTER TO CHASE THE ONES YOU BELIEVE IN.

By the time I'd returned to my sister's house, having covered what felt like the entirety of Austin proper, she was ready for me.

"Want to talk?" she asked, in a voice more protective than worried. So I let it all out. The whole story.

Everything up to that point, including all my doubts and fears and frustrations.

And my sister, being the wise, soulful woman she is, took it all in and said, "What these women have been forced to endure was wrong. And it sounds to me like they need your help."

And then she did what all good preachers do. She said, "Let's pray on it." And she prayed over me. She asked God to look out for her brother, to look out for the firm, but mostly to watch over the survivors. "God," she said, "please allow your will to be done."

And in that moment, I started thinking about all that she's done for her congregation over the years. That was her flock. Those were the people she served. Maybe, just maybe, this was my flock. She's been called to protect her people. Maybe I was being called to protect a different set of strangers who needed their own guidance.

This was not the time, as my father once said, to be mediocre. So I phoned our head of litigation, Andy Rubenstein, and said, "Andy, we can't let this case go. We are sitting on something that can genuinely change lives. These women need help. I know other firms don't think it's worth the risk, but I know it's worth the risk. We're moving forward with this, even if we have to do it alone."

To which Andy said, "I'm with you, Darren—100 percent—but if we go at this alone, how the hell are we going to raise enough money to fight USC?"

CHAPTER 6

BATTLE PLANS

PUT IN THE WORK, AND THE MONEY WILL FOLLOW

Had I drawn up a to-do list, in the early summer of 2018, regarding our work on the USC case, it would have looked something like this:

- Committed to doing the right thing? Check.

- Assembled a skilled team? Check.

- Performed enough due diligence and in-depth research? Check.

- Devised a battle plan? Check.

- Compiled necessary funds? Empty glaringly unchecked box.

It was that last bullet point that everyone inside our firm seemed to be most worried about. In the early going, everywhere I turned I was greeted with some variation of that same question.

Darren, where's the money coming from?

Darren, can we actually afford to take on this case?

Darren, a word, if I may, about how we're actually going to pay for this.

A quick note about capital. If you're a plaintiff-side mass-tort attorney, your opponents will always have more money at their disposal than you will. This is an indisputable fact, which you might as well come to grips with from the jump.

Whenever I talk to other lawyers about our long-standing battles against deep-pocketed defendants, my mind invariably coils back to my high school years in Katy, Texas. I was surrounded by kids whose parents had a lot more money than my family did. They lived in bigger homes, wore more expensive clothes, and drove cars I'd only seen on television and giant billboards.

Nevertheless, I also recognized very early on that I possessed something that most of my peers lacked: grit.

Most people will tell you that poor or middle-class kids who attend an affluent high school is a tough draw. I say it's just the opposite. For me, it was an advantage because it taught me to never, ever, take money or opportunities for granted.

The truth is, I think a lot of my high school peers were spoiled rotten. I could tell, even back then, that they didn't appreciate the security and opportunities they'd been given.

Case in point, I asked a friend of mine one summer what he was going to do over his break. He groaned and told me that his "old man" was pushing him to intern at his law firm. My friend was having none of it. "If he thinks I'm going to spend my summer break working at a law office," he said, "he's nuts."

My face, on the other hand, lit up like the North Star. Internship? At a law firm? With a well-respected lawyer? I immediately tried to broker a deal. "Well, if you don't want to take him up on his offer, can I interview for the job?"

Initially, my friend looked at me like I was from another planet, but he also recognized that this was a golden opportunity to weasel his way out of work for the next three months.

Cut to my friend spending that summer stoned out of his mind and me working my ass off for his dad. I told my friend's father I'd come to his firm to learn. As far as I was concerned, there was no job too small for me to take on. Want me to sharpen pencils? Fine. Want me to field phone calls? Not a problem.

I had only one caveat: he had to mentor me and help me to upload as much knowledge as I possibly could while I was under his employ.

I'll never forget the look on his face when he realized I actually meant it. That I'd gladly handle every task he put in front of me. Over time, his suspicion morphed into something approaching genuine respect because I treated every task like it was a final exam. Easy tasks. Complex ones. Small cases. Big ones. It didn't matter. I gave 110 percent regardless of the job.

In return, I was given a taste of my future profession. We may not currently handle a large number of real estate cases at D. Miller & Associates, PLLC, but that formative experience assured me that I was on the right track. Becoming a lawyer was no longer a childhood fantasy.

I realized that I actually enjoyed doing the work. All of the work. The people and the paperwork. The legal minutiae and the financial planning. The small Pyrrhic victories and the consequential ones.

Here's the thing: everyone wants to be a home run hitter. Doesn't matter what profession you're in; everybody dreams of hitting the long ball. If you're in sales, you want to close the mega deal. If you're a trader, you thirst for the quick ten-bagger. If you're a movie director, you dream about making the highest-grossing blockbuster of all time.

Lawyers are no different, especially mass-tort lawyers. Most of us are hardwired to swing for the fences. We want the hundred-million-dollar settlements—or better yet the billion-dollar jaw-droppers.

Trust me—there's no greater rush in life than handing a seven-figure check to a deserving client. It's an electric moment. Shock meets elation. Relief and tears and gratitude and pride all pressed into a tiny slip of paper.

Here's the twist though. Successful firms, like ours, don't swing for the fences every time we're up to bat. To hit the occasional grand slam, we play a lot of small ball in between.

SUCCESSFUL FIRMS, LIKE OURS, DON'T SWING FOR THE FENCES EVERY TIME WE'RE UP TO BAT. TO HIT THE OCCASIONAL GRAND SLAM, WE PLAY A LOT OF SMALL BALL IN BETWEEN.

I have no problem—in fact, I still really enjoy—taking on personal-injury cases because those are the cases that helped establish our firm's sterling reputation. I'll gladly string together a couple singles. I'll take that well-timed double. And the occasional triple. Because the revenue we generate from those personal-injury cases allows us to take a swing at a case like USC when it comes along.

There are some mass-tort firms that have become so big they won't even consider taking on anything but mass torts. We ascribe to a different model. When it comes to good cases, we don't discriminate. Slip and falls. Eighteen-wheelers. Car accidents. If it's a quality case that can help out someone in need, we will consider it.

I firmly believe that our commitment to maintaining a "balanced portfolio" of cases has allowed us to hit home runs like USC.

This is why, when everyone was sweating over how we were going to raise enough money to pursue USC, I responded with a very simple answer: We'll keep doing what we've always done. We will make it happen!

Here's the bittersweet truth about running your own law firm. You may get paid the most, but you also get paid last, which explains why I hold so firmly to one of my personal mantras: don't make excuses; just make it happen.

I might not be the same kid I was in high school, but I'm still the guy who's going to forego a chill summer to reap greater benefits in the fall.

Same goes for the way I run my firm. Rather than write myself a big fat bonus check every time I win a case, I've learned the importance of reinvesting those profits into major torts like USC.

In order to take on USC, I knew we'd have to spend a lot of money.

We draft very detailed budgets at our firm. We've built a top-flight in-house accounting team to take a jeweler's loupe to every single potential line item, as well as carefully track our spending throughout the tort. And I wholeheartedly recommend you do the same.

When I ran the numbers, I estimated that we'd need northward of one million dollars to properly handle a case of this magnitude.

We decided to allocate funds to achieve each of the following:

- Run social media advertising campaigns to acquire more clients

- Boost our hiring budgets to bring in new lawyers and team members

- Cover as many flights as we'd need to fly back and forth from Houston to California

- Hire a media consultant to aid us in gaining media attention
- Fund all our necessary casework, including depositions, trial prep, hearings, etc.

I did not, however, have a million dollars stashed away in a rainy day fund. It was time to put up or shut up. I said to myself, "Make no excuses, Darren. Just make it happen."

So one morning, I gathered my team together and made a quick announcement. "Raising the money we need for this case," I reiterated, "is my responsibility. You do your job; I'll take care of mine. Period. End of story. Now, let's get to work."

Old-school financial discipline never hurt anyone. We weren't going to be greedy. We were going to be judicious in how much money we spent and where we spent it. But most importantly, we were going to lean into the process we'd already established.

I'd raise the necessary money by continuing to build a diversified portfolio of cases, which leaned on both personal-injury cases and mass torts.

The truth is the scared money rarely wins, whether you're running a business or a law firm. I've always considered myself an entrepreneur who happens to practice law, not the other way around, which is an important distinction because lawyers, by definition, are notoriously inflexible when it comes to building a successful practice.

The skills required to be a first-rate legal scholar or brilliant courtroom tactician don't automatically translate into being a financially successful lawyer. When it comes to money, most lawyers consider themselves financially savvy but wind up wasting their money.

To protect the guilty, I'll refrain from recounting too many stories, but most of these mistakes are rooted in one cardinal flaw:

lawyers are creatures of habit. The prospect of breaking from their rigidly established routines absolutely terrifies them.

As any successful business executive will tell you, when it comes to money, capital is hard to make and easy to lose. What you earn today can be just as easily lost tomorrow if you don't keep pace with the times.

I'd argue, for instance, that every lawyer reading this book—whether you're focused on bankruptcy issues, real estate, personal injuries, or disability benefits—should have some exposure to mass torts in their portfolio.

Choosing an appropriate mix is up to you. I'm not saying that 80 percent of your portfolio should be composed of mass torts. Nor am I saying you should play it too safe and cap it at 2 percent. But every day that goes by where you don't have any mass torts on your docket is a missed opportunity.

Here's a simple analogy: Successful lawyers fly first class. Successful mass-tort lawyers own their own airplanes.

It all comes back to those three magical letters: ROI. Your return on investment.

The ROI on a successful mass-tort case can be incredibly lucrative. Let's do some simple back-of-the-envelope math to prove it. Say you're a personal-injury lawyer. How much money do you earn on a typical car-wreck case? Maybe $8,000 in attorneys' fees.

Now work backward from there. How much did you have to spend to acquire that case and see it to completion? Maybe $2,000 or $3,000. Congratulations. You brought home $5,000 in profit on that one case.

Now, let's run the numbers on a mass-tort case involving Roundup. Our cost of acquisition for each client for that case was $1,800 per person. Let's say we spent, on average, another $1,000 to properly vet each potential client (i.e., we ensured that their particular type of cancer and their symptoms aligned with the parameters of the tort).

We settled, on average, each of our Roundup clients' cases for $80,000 per client. Sixty percent of the settlement went to the plaintiff, and 40 percent went to us in the form of attorneys' fees. That works out to roughly $32,000 per case.

That's simple math, isn't it? The tort yielded us $32,000 per client, and your car-wreck case netted you $5,000 dollars. That's a huge difference, right?

But don't forget to multiply that $32,000 figure times the number of clients we represented. Pick a figure. Let's say fifty clients total. That translates to $1.6 million. And if we were to represent one hundred clients using this average payout, that figure jumps to $3.2 million.

The order of operations, no matter the tort, goes something like this: Take your available capital. Spend it to find clients. And reap unprecedented financial rewards.

It's a no-brainer, right? This isn't a magic trick. Every time I present case studies like these at conferences, people can't believe their eyes.

And then what happens? They go home, they settle back into their routine, and the next thing you know they're talking themselves out of a perfectly rational business decision.

It's absolutely baffling because our portfolio of personal-injury cases at D. Miller & Associates, PLLC, doesn't look much different from yours. If you're a successful lawyer—no matter your focus—you possess the skill sets needed to be successful in mass torts. Chances are, you know how to multitask. You know how to acquire clients. You know how to efficiently process cases. And you certainly know how to talk to and strike deals with other lawyers.

The only difference between you and me is that I recognized the value of using the profits I've accrued from our personal-injury work to regularly fund our mass-tort work. It's not a question of changing your ways as much as using one revenue stream to fuel a second, far more lucrative one.

If you fear the word "change," as so many lawyers do, try not to think of it in those terms. Chalk it up as a necessary business expense. You're simply applying what you already know to a different subset of clients and reaping the end rewards.

So when people try to scare you and say, "It takes a lot of money to take on a mass-tort case," recognize that they are telling the truth. But also keep in mind that you won't be writing a single $1 million check at the beginning of each tort.

You can amortize the costs of your torts over time. And if you continue to leverage your skill sets, you'll see an ROI on your investment that will change your life.

I guarantee it.

As I always tell my team, you never know how or when your next great case will cross your radar.

Even though we started hitting home runs by representing clients in mass torts involving major players like BP and Bayer, on cases involving oil spills and products like Yaz birth control pills, I never lost focus of where I came from or why I'd chosen to become a lawyer in the first place.

In many ways, I'm still that same little kid sitting in a London living room watching episodes of *Petrocelli* on TV and thinking, "I can use my law degree to help the overlooked and neglected. The people who've been gobbled up and spit out by this world."

I think it's easy to forget that—to overlook the small cases to chase the big ones. I see it all the time, sometimes even from people on my own team. They'll tell me, "Oh, that's a slip-and-fall case—we don't have time to talk to them."

My response is "The hell you don't." Don't tell me you're above any case or anyone. You don't have time for leg injuries? C'mon. You have the time.

I'm not saying you have to take every case presented to you, but I do believe that you have a responsibility to point people in the right direction. You're a counselor, so counsel people.

It doesn't take much effort for you to say something like, "I'm really sorry this happened to you. I can't help you, but here's what I recommend you do, or here's someone you might want to see. And if you ever need our services in the future, call this number."

It's my firm's belief that money is a by-product of success. It's a by-product of taking care of people. Your clients. Your team. Your community.

Once you fall down the dangerous rabbit hole of focusing exclusively on making money, you're setting yourself up for abject failure in the long run.

If you grade your worth—as a lawyer, a person, a professional— on how much money you make, your ego is going to swallow you whole. And when that happens, otherwise smart lawyers start doing some very stupid and vile things.

It all comes down to relationships. Be a lawyer, damn it. Is that so hard? When you close a case, call your client back and say, "Even though we took care of this issue, I'm still your lawyer. I still want to be your lawyer. If you ever have any questions, don't hesitate to reach out."

This begs the question, Have you done your absolute best to build strong long-term relationships with every potential client who has crossed your path?

I ask myself that question as often as I can. Because ultimately it's the relationships we forge with everyday people—the people who so many white-shoe law firms view as disposable—that ensure our firm's phones never stop ringing. Every day. Every week. Every month. Every year.

That's our secret sauce—one of the enduring keys to our success. We take quality cases, big and small. That's how a small Texas firm amassed the guts and the financial resources to take on one of the most powerful universities in the country.

We refused to make excuses. Instead, we put in the work. We built up our savings, keeping our powder dry until we could set it ablaze when the revolution came calling.

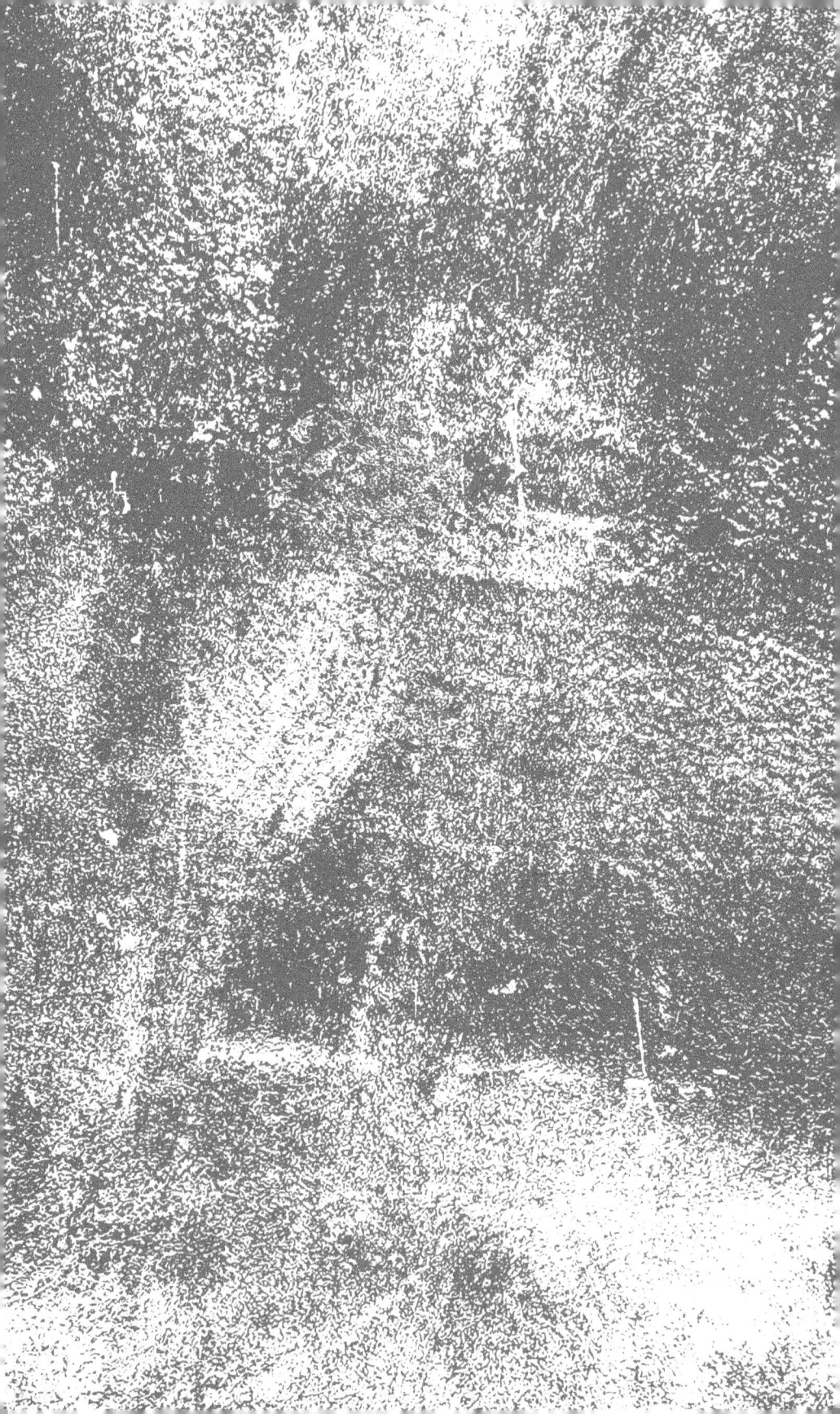

CHAPTER 7

SOCIAL STUDIES

THE ART AND CRAFT OF CLIENT ACQUISITION

I realize what I'm about to recommend will be as comforting to some people as recommending a root canal. However, in our line of work, there's just no getting around the fact that you have to spend money to make even more money.

Forget location, location, location. These days, it's all about marketing, marketing, marketing. Clients aren't going to magically find you. You have to go out into the world—the digital world—and make sure they find you. To achieve that goal and to build a fully vetted docket of mass-tort clients requires real capital.

If you're more of an idealist, as I am, think of it this way: there's strength in numbers. When it comes to mass torts, the more clients you can convince to join a particular tort, the more concerned the defense will likely become.

Do you want to attract media attention? Do you want to enable your clients' stories to see the light of a television screen? Do you want to ensure, after years of being muzzled, that your clients stop being marginalized and start being heard?

Then go out and spend an appropriate amount of money to ensure that's the case. Spread it all around. Invest in your website, launch Facebook ads, create YouTube videos. Let everyone know that you've picked a side. And then invite others to join that movement.

The key is to be strategic about how you deploy your marketing dollars. When it comes to acquiring mass-tort clients, I say, "Forget the billboards. Forget the radio ads. Forget the flyers." It's better to go where all the eyeballs are—straight into people's social media feeds.

I used to be a big-data skeptic. Now I'm a true believer. I've seen, firsthand, just how effective social media advertising can be when it's deployed the right way. Take, for example, the tragic events that occurred on October 1, 2017, when a gunman, perched from a window on the thirty-second floor of the Mandalay Resort in Las Vegas, took the lives of more than fifty people and injured 850 others who were attending a nearby music festival.

Let's say you saw that case the same way my firm did. That you believed MGM Resorts International could have done much more to prevent that tragedy from occurring—and that everyone who attended that concert deserved representation and restitution.

How would you go about finding those potential clients?

Sounds prohibitively expensive, right? Oh, but it wasn't. Within hours of the shooting, we reached out to one of the best social media advertisers in our industry, Jacob Malherbe of X Social Media.

Years ago, Jacob taught me the golden rule of social media advertising: the faster you start searching for potential clients, the less money you'll need to find them. The early bird, it turns out, gets all the clients.

In terms of the Las Vegas shooter case, the math worked out something like this: If we deployed a Facebook ad campaign right away, we would pay $30 to $50 per lead. Wait a few weeks, and we were looking at a price tag of $500 per lead. Dillydally any longer, and it would've cost us $1,000 or more to track down those same individuals.

So naturally, we acted quickly. Jacob deployed a brilliant campaign that used geo-targeting to pin the area surrounding the concert venue. He then coupled that initial search by using something he calls his Time Machine application, which enabled him to ask Facebook to send targeted ads to people who'd recently visited that exact location.

Soon, we were signing up eight clients *per day*. We vetted them and welcomed them to our firm. In 2019, a settlement was announced for the case: $800 million was split between more than four thousand plaintiffs.

Let me make one thing clear: there's absolutely nothing preventing any attorney—whether you're a bankruptcy, real estate, or personal-injury lawyer—from jumping into the mass-tort space and winning similar victories.

How exactly, you might be asking, does one do that?

Remember, you don't have to be a trial lawyer to become a mass-tort lawyer. Trial lawyers are responsible for litigation. In order to present the best possible case, they need options, the opportunity to sift through hundreds—and sometimes thousands—of individual plaintiffs and cherry-pick those who have the most compelling stories. A trial lawyer can then present those stories to the courts to build the strongest case possible.

It's just common sense. Which option would give you a better chance of winning: relying solely on the people who just happen to retain your firm's services or having the freedom to select from an expansive pool of a thousand-plus clients?

This brings me to a dirty little secret about mass-tort firms. We often rely on smaller firms to help us build larger dockets. Think of it this way: Tier 1 firms—sometimes referred to as handling firms—have the ability to not only acquire cases but litigate them. However, all of us want—and in some cases need—other lawyers to bring us fully vetted clients so we can represent the largest number of clients possible.

Just as no single lawyer can perform all the legwork necessary to exhaustively research a case, no single firm, no matter how powerful, is capable of finding and signing every potential victim in a mass tort, especially one like USC, which stretched back decades.

Most attorneys don't have the experience to become mass-tort trial lawyers, but they can quickly and easily transition into being what we call originating partners.

Originating partners are lawyers who find, vet, and acquire clients and then hand over the rights to represent those clients to larger and more-experienced handling firms. In exchange, originating partners earn a percentage of the tier 1 firm's overall attorneys' fees. This joint-venture relationship benefits both parties, in that the originating partner can just sit back and allow us to handle all the hard work involved with litigating the case and winning the actual settlement.

What do we, as a handling firm, get out of the exchange? A bigger piece of the overall settlement.

As one might expect, trial lawyers and handling firms take home a larger percentage of the overall settlement than the originating partner. We take 40 percent in attorneys' fees from the monetary settlements won by each plaintiff in the tort. Whereas an originating lawyer tends to take home anywhere from 25 to 50 percent of the attorneys' fees captured by the handling firm.

Once proceedings begin, trial lawyers need to step in and litigate. Originating partners, by contrast, simply wait for settlements or judgments. Should the plaintiffs succeed in their suit, acquisitions lawyers will collect their cut and go on their merry way, sometimes having offered very little litigation support to the case.

At D. Miller & Associates, PLLC, we sometimes assume the role of a handling firm. And in other instances, we are perfectly content to be an originating partner and allow another firm to litigate the case.

When we assume the role of an originating partner, we often demand 50 percent of a firm's total attorneys' fees. But if you're new to the space, that percentage is likely to be closer to 25 or 30 percent.

This is why it's so important to partner with the *right* handling firm. It all comes down to building long-term relationships. When we commit to a tort, our partners can rest assured that we will do everything in our power to maximize the amount of the final settlement.

Other firms are perfectly content to accept lowball settlements. It all comes down to differing definitions of value. How much value will a handling firm place on your client's injuries?

Never align yourself with a firm that's willing to settle for small, underwhelming settlements. If anything, it's often best for new mass-tort lawyers to partner with a handling firm that provides a lower fee split but fights to win a larger settlement. After all, would you rather have 30 percent of $1 million or 40 percent of $250,000?

Whichever path you choose, it's absolutely critical that you leverage your internal marketing efforts and rely on outside advertising vendors to find, vet, and sign clients.

Don't sell yourself short. If you're an excellent bankruptcy lawyer, then continue to be an excellent bankruptcy lawyer. Keep doing what you do best, but remember that you can diversify your practice, at very little risk, if you go out and allocate enough money to finding clients.

And when I use the phrase "spend money," you have to do more than simply keep the office paper clip jar fully stocked. You need to spend some serious money.

My advice? Leverage *every* media channel you can. Create your own YouTube videos. Stock your website with targeted news stories, blog entries, and research. Launch separate online landing pages where you can vet potential clients by asking them a series of initial questions. Hire outside social media experts to deploy targeted advertisements.

The goal is to quickly dial up an all-out media blitz.

Why the rush? Because once word slips that a mass tort is heating up, it becomes an all-out race to find clients. The key is to seize the first-mover advantage. Don't wait for the starter pistol to go off. Be the starter pistol. Start searching right away because this first-mover advantage puts the burden on everyone else to try and catch up and close the lead you've already established.

THE KEY IS TO SEIZE THE FIRST-MOVER ADVANTAGE. DON'T WAIT FOR THE STARTER PISTOL TO GO OFF.

As far as I'm concerned, social media advertising isn't a luxury; it's become a prerequisite for survival in our field. To illustrate why this is the case, I hope you'll indulge me in recounting a short parable about a lawyer who did the opposite.

Remember that old book *All I Really Need to Know I Learned in Kindergarten*? One day I'm going to write a quasi sequel for young lawyers. It's going to be entitled *Everything I Learned Not to Do from Incompetent Lawyers*.

Let me go back in time to when I was a recent law school graduate. I was eager, perhaps a little too eager, to make a name for myself, so I agreed to work for a smaller personal-injury law firm that inadvertently provided me a master class in how not to run a law firm.

The truth is I think this individual (who I'll call the Great Lawyer) might have been too old—too set in his ways—to see that the world was passing him by. I've since met a thousand lawyers like him. Slow moving as a World War II submarine. Averse to change and miles behind the curve.

At one point, I decided I'd seen enough. I just couldn't take it anymore. During one of the Great Lawyer's extended lunch breaks, I snuck out and started passing out our business cards at offices and apartment complexes across the city. I didn't have much to offer other than my sincere promise that our firm wanted to help. I promised free consultations and free referrals. And if anyone had questions, of any kind, we'd answer them free of charge.

In the end, the Great Lawyer wasn't happy with my hustle—and let me know in no uncertain terms that he was content with running his office the way he'd always run the office. So I did the only logical thing—I quit.

If there was a silver lining to all this, it's that I convinced one of his young paralegals to come work for me as my head paralegal. She worked as my trusted jack-of-all-trades for more than a decade. Although she eventually went to go work for another firm, we enjoy a friendly and mutually beneficial relationship to this day.

But the time I spent with the Great Lawyer taught me an invaluable business lesson: anyone who does the same thing over and over again and expects different results is guaranteed to fail.

If your firm is relying on the same tired client-acquisitions strategies—the billboards, the newspaper ads, the cheap flyers pinned to coffeehouse billboards—that everyone was still using five years ago (or God forbid ten years ago), you're going to end up like my old employer: belly-up and broke.

I say this with all due respect to the old-timers: Don't be a dinosaur. Don't fall so far behind the digital curve that you'll need a time machine to make things right.

DON'T BE A DINOSAUR. DON'T FALL SO FAR BEHIND THE DIGITAL CURVE THAT YOU'LL NEED A TIME MACHINE TO MAKE THINGS RIGHT.

In terms of our work on the USC case, I knew the moment I heard Betty's story that there had to be other women who'd been abused by the same doctor. There had to be women scattered across the country—and as we'd later discover, the globe—who wanted to share their stories but had never been given an opportunity to do so.

It takes courage for someone like our early USC client, Betty, to light the flame, and it's our job as attorneys to keep stoking that fire—adding more stories to that blaze—so that perpetrators of these crimes understand they can no longer suppress the truth.

Our firm promised Betty we would build a mass-tort suit around her, and we did just that by taking all the research we'd compiled—as well as all that we were learning about the #MeToo movement—and using it to build marketing campaigns that were both fact driven and deeply emotional.

When you're dealing with an issue as complex as sexual abuse, survivors can sniff out sleazy lawyers and opportunists a mile away. The first thing that our brilliant marketing director, Mari Balentina, asked her team to do was put themselves in the shoes of women like Betty.

The three keywords she kept reiterating, day after day, were "informative," "sensitive," and "empathetic." Every single marketing piece we produced, whether it was a YouTube video or a tweet, had to be vetted to ensure they embodied those three attributes.

We started with unassailable facts. Did our work present enough hard news and verified statistics that a trusted news organization would air them? If it failed this initial test, we quickly scrapped the ad and went back to the drawing board.

When it came to the tone and voice of our ads, we gained people's trust by refusing to hide our righteous outrage. At the same time, we were very sensitive to the fact that stepping forward to relive old traumas would not be easy.

I vividly recall one of the first ads we launched on YouTube that June. Over time, some of our clients would say it resonated deeply with them, as it did with me the moment Mari screened it for us.

It opened with a dark shade of red, followed by the gradual appearance of a woman's dark silhouette. We didn't want to use any generic stock photos because we wanted the ad to speak to every potential survivor—every race, creed, age, and ethnicity—and capture the diverse range of people who'd been abused.

Mari volunteered to do the voice-over work herself. She began by listing a series of facts. According to a recent survey, nearly 30 percent of female undergrads had reported falling victim to some form of sexual abuse or misconduct.

Then we quickly transitioned to a short timeline recounting key events that had recently occurred at USC, including the recent resignation of a key university administrator.

This hard-news focus then shifted into a direct address to viewers. The ad said, "If you were treated by Dr. Tyndall at any point from 1989 to 2017, you may be one of many survivors entitled to compensation."

We made it clear that we saw it as our mission to help survivors share their stories. Our ad spoke directly and honestly to potential clients about the fear they might feel in coming forward, as well as the overall trauma of sexual abuse. It offered a promise that we would do everything in our power to fight for them and help them find justice.

The ad ended with a simple coda: "We know you are hurt. We don't want you to stand alone."

I think sincerity has always been one of our firm's secret weapons. I think we hire people who sincerely want to help other people. But it wasn't until I saw that ad that I realized just how important it was for us to embed those emotions in our marketing efforts.

Our USC ads resonated because we were so sincere in our delivery. We didn't shoot from the hip; we shot from the heart. Every single member of our firm had done their research. They'd read the testimonies. They'd educated themselves. Thus, we were prepared to help bring these stories from the shadows into the light.

We spent the money required to get the job done. We launched a multipronged marketing effort. Every single line of content was handed over to our social media, digital, and website teams to ensure it was seen and optimized for the right audiences.

Mari demanded depth and breadth. We wrote stories and blog posts for our website, which became a de facto news feed for issues related to the #MeToo movement and the USC case. We created special graphics and launched our own suite of Facebook ads while simultaneously hiring Jacob Malherbe and X Social Media to deploy their own ads on Facebook.

Every time someone clicked on one of our ads, they were directed to an online landing page, which asked them a series of questions to ensure they qualified for the tort.

If they passed, they received a phone call from our head litigator, Andy Rubenstein, who created a second questionnaire to drill deeper into everyone's story to weed out any fake stories.

I wish things were different, but it's not uncommon for people to provide false answers on a web form. So mass-tort firms have to double back around and ask more detailed questions.

Given all the research Andy had already accumulated, he was able to filter through these contacts and find clients whose stories and experiences could be verified.

I talked to every single one of our USC clients. I was able to forge a lasting connection, to listen again, and to give a preview as to what might follow as the case progressed.

And rather quickly our client list grew. It was astounding how many people Dr. Tyndall had abused. I don't have the words to describe the tidal wave of emotions that we all experienced. Shock. Surprise. Heartbreak.

It was in that moment, after listening to so many women's stories, that we realized we really were part of a much larger movement. It wasn't just #MeToo. It was *us too*.

We expected to find a number of additional clients, but when the number reached almost 150, our surprise turned temporarily to sorrow. A sadness that perhaps we all could have done more much sooner.

Nevertheless, years from now, when I am old and gray, I know without question that the money we spent to find these women and give them a voice will be some of the best money we have ever spent.

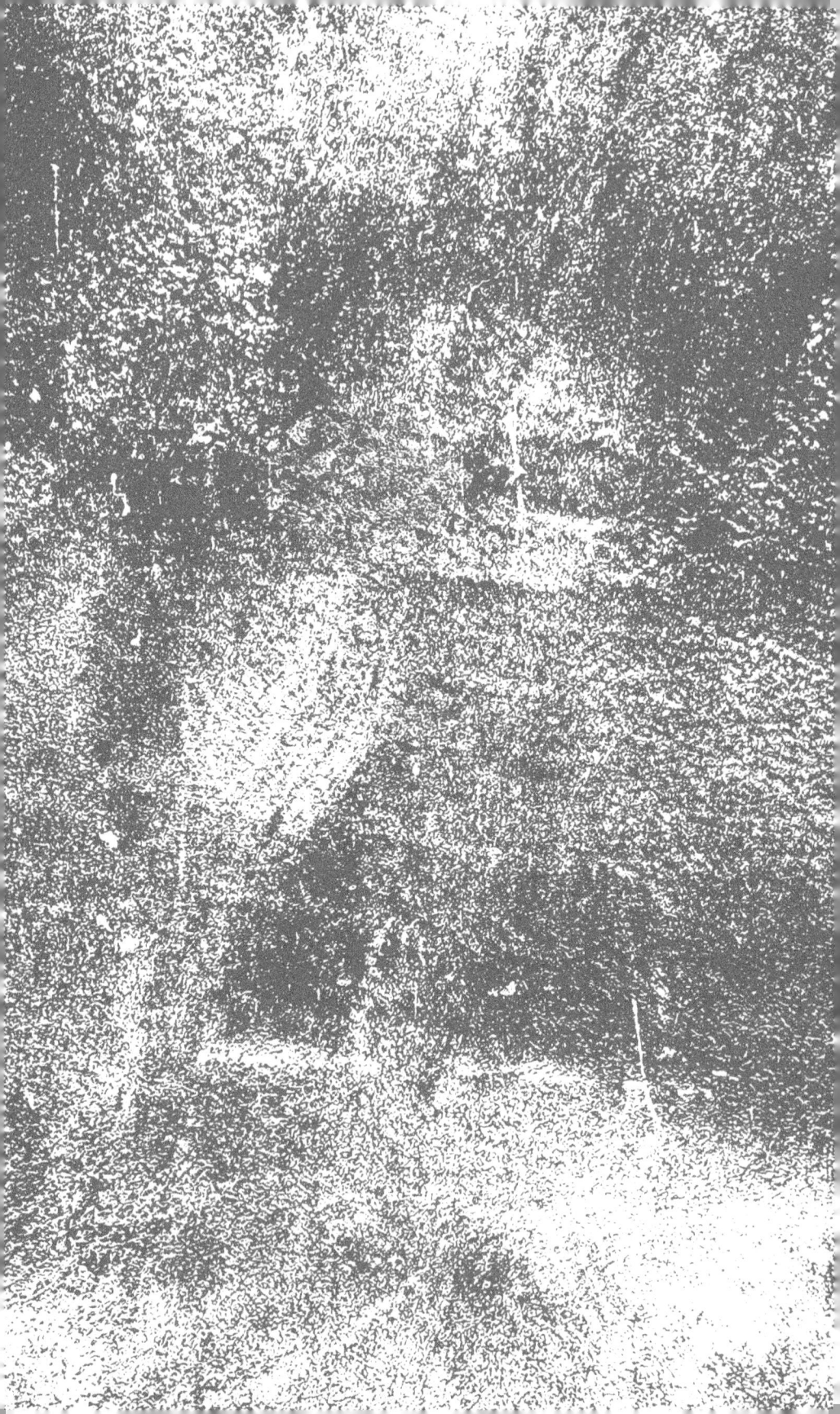

CHAPTER 8

A CRISIS MANAGEMENT PRIMER

SHOW SOME (TOUGH) LOVE

My phone rings again. It's a call from our head litigator, Andy Ruben-stein. I smile. Andy is one of the best in our business. He's intelligent, business savvy, and extremely devoted to his family. He's my right-hand man in more ways than one.

Andy and I go back more than twenty years. When I decided to strike out on my own, he took me under his wing, schooling me on how to extract the maximum amount of value from every case that came across my desk.

It wasn't just what he taught me; it was the way he taught me. Most lawyers think they're smooth operators, but Andy is an extremely engaging conversationalist, who's proven himself, time and time again, to be someone who trusts and can be trusted.

In addition, we share the belief that the more organized the lawyer, the more relaxed the client will be when providing depositions or being interviewed in front of a TV camera. As a result, he's fastidious in his case prep, his media prep, and his witness prep, which explains why Andy has such a sterling track record of delivering steady six-figure and seven-figure settlements.

I'm fortunate to have him on our team, and our clients are fortunate to have him representing them. At this point, Andy and I have been working together so long we can finish each other's sentences.

Most days, that is.

Today seems to be an exception.

When I see my cell phone buzz and his name appear, I immediately slide my thumb across my screen and start speaking before he can say a single word. "That was fast," I say. "You made it to Los Angeles already?"

I listen for a beat. My smile cracks, like a snapped rubber band. This is not good.

Andy's voice sounds harried, a little panicked. He never sounds like this. Ever.

"Darren," he says, "I'm not getting on that plane. We're not ready for this. We need more time."

What? My eyes shoot toward my watch. I curl my wrist to check the exact time.

This is really *not* good.

I know where Andy *should* be. He should be sauntering down the center aisle of a parked airplane, unloading his carry-on baggage into an overhead compartment and buckling up for his flight to Los Angeles with our marketing director, Mari Balentina.

Everyone in our firm knows the importance of Andy making his flight. We've been planning his trip for days, in part because producers of two different programs, *Nightline* and *Good Morning America*, have contacted us and want to interview four of our clients for a piece about Dr. Tyndall and the USC case.

To secure this all-important interview, Andy needs to fly to Los Angeles, as quickly as possible, and formally file our lawsuit against USC. Our decision, weeks earlier, to hire a media-consulting firm was paying real dividends. Our new partner was educating us about the inner workings of West Coast media outlets and helped us select women from our client list who were best suited to sit down for extended media interviews.

We learned a great deal that summer, which is why I encourage ambitious firms to always devote a part of their budgets to hiring seasoned media consultants. We learned how to pitch our clients' stories, where to pitch them (as it turns out, the London West Hollywood hotel is where everyone who's anyone seems to organize press conferences), and how, generally speaking, to talk to the media.

Reputable news programs, like *Nightline* and *Good Morning America*, aren't interested in reading informal complaints and demand letters. If they are going to devote airtime to a mass-tort case, they want to see physical lawsuits, stamped and approved, before they proceed.

In terms of media attention, the tide was beginning to turn. More mainstream press outlets were showing interest in the USC story. I think an extraordinary amount of credit must be given to the *Los Angeles Times*, which published a damning exposé of Dr. Tyndall and USC on May 16, 2018.

It was an extremely well-researched story,[4] which pulled evidence from hundreds of documents and relied on interviews with more than twenty current and former USC employees.

That astounding piece, the first story in an ongoing series that would earn the paper a Pulitzer, was the first major news article to shine a dim yet powerful light on Dr. Tyndall's abuse, as well as the negligent decisions made behind closed doors at the university.

The story outlined a clear pattern of abuse and wanton indifference to the doctor's misdeeds, which had clearly stretched back decades. The paper interviewed numerous members of Dr. Tyndall's staff, who made it clear that they'd voiced serious concerns to the university about what they'd witnessed during his exams.

Tyndall, it seemed, had developed a reputation for photographing students' genitalia, allegations that were corroborated by students and staff.[5] Others came forward to recount chilling stories of seeing Tyndall inappropriately touch patients, including inserting his fingers into women's vaginas and making sexually suggestive remarks during questionable pelvic exams.

It seemed to be widely known within the corridors of power at USC that Dr. Tyndall paid special attention to certain female patients—specifically women who exhibited a limited understanding of English or those who were seeing a gynecologist for the first time.

The piece also included a shocking story from 2016, which involved, of all things, an infestation of fruit flies that had colonized Tyndall's office. Determined to curb a larger outbreak, staff members entered his office to find that the flies had gathered around a rotten

4   Harriet Ryan, Matt Hamilton, and Paul Pringle, "A USC Doctor Was Accused of Bad Behavior with Young Women for Years. The University Let Him Continue Treating Students," *Los Angeles Times*, May 16, 2018, https://www.latimes.com/local/california/la-me-usc-doctor-misconduct-complaints-20180515-story.html.

5   Harriet Ryan and Matt Hamilton, "USC's Controversial $215-Million Settlement with Gynecologist's Victims Moves Forward," *Los Angeles Times*, February 12, 2019, https://www.latimes.com/local/lanow/la-me-ln-usc-settlement-lawsuits-former-patient-gynecologist-20190213-story.html.

sack of fruit left under his desk. Nearby sat a box filled with photographs of women's genitalia.[6]

What USC did next is still open to debate, but shortly thereafter Dr. Tyndall formally resigned from his position. The date was June 30, 2017.[7]

A year later, in May 2018, USC president C. L. "Max" Nikias also announced he would be stepping down from his post.[8] By the end of that same month, the Los Angeles Police Department was actively investigating dozens of complaints filed by former patients of Dr. Tyndall,[9] a number that would further mushroom with each passing month.[10]

I realized that if we didn't act immediately—if we didn't file our suit and jump at the opportunity to share these women's stories—USC might, once again, weasel its way out of taking responsibility for these heinous crimes.

As you might expect, everyone in our firm had been burning the midnight oil leading up to Andy's flight to Los Angeles. Our clients had done their part; now it was time for us to do ours.

I think it's universally true, for all lawyers, that the more you care about a case, the more you feel the weight of the world bearing down

---

6   Harriet Ryan, Matt Hamilton, and Paul Pringle, "A USC Doctor Was Accused of Bad Behavior with Young Women for Years. The University Let Him Continue Treating Students," *Los Angeles Times*, May 16, 2018, https://www.latimes.com/local/california/la-me-usc-doctor-misconduct-complaints-20180515-story.html.

7   Ibid.

8   Matt Hamilton, Harriet Ryan, Paul Pringle, and Steve Lopez, "USC President C. L. Max Nikias to Step Down," May 25, 2018, https://www.latimes.com/local/lanow/la-me-max-nikias-usc-20180525-story.html.

9   Matt Hamilton, Richard Winton, and Adam Elmahrek, "LAPD Begins Sweeping Criminal Probe of Former USC Gynecologist While Urging Patients to Come Forward," *Los Angeles Times*, May 29, 2018, https://www.latimes.com/local/lanow/la-me-usc-tyndall-lapd-20180529-story.html.

10   Matt Hamilton and Harriet Ryan, "Ex-USC Gynecologist Retains High-Profile Criminal Attorney," *Los Angeles Times*, July 13, 2018, https://www.latimes.com/local/lanow/la-me-ln-usc-gynecologist-defense-lawyer-20180713-story.html.

on you as it progresses. As a mass-tort lawyer, the thing you fear most of all is disappointing your clients.

And that pressure can take a real and lasting toll on anyone, even the strongest among us.

We've all been there, haven't we? I've certainly been there. I can vividly remember the mix of emotions coursing through my body when I began prepping to take

I THINK IT'S UNIVERSALLY TRUE, FOR ALL LAWYERS, THAT THE MORE YOU CARE ABOUT A CASE, THE MORE YOU FEEL THE WEIGHT OF THE WORLD BEARING DOWN ON YOU AS IT PROGRESSES.

the Texas bar. I wanted to make my family proud. And I was crushed to learn, upon taking the test for the first time, that I'd failed.

I'd never failed anything in my life up to that point. I'd cruised through my MBA program at the University of St. Thomas. I'd excelled at Thurgood Marshall School of Law. And I was so confident that I'd ace the bar exam that I proactively joined a friend's law office.

I was stunned, mostly because I was disappointed in myself. Disappointed that I didn't push myself to study a little harder and be more prepared. I remember telling everyone in my family that the next time around, things would be different. But much to my shock, once again, the results wound up being the same.

I'd now failed the bar exam twice.

Around that time, I received a phone call from my father. I was living with two friends, Chris Budak and Lee Ford, in West Houston at the time.

"Darren," he said, "I want you to drive out to our house in Cypress. I want to talk to you about something." So I buckled up and drove over to see him. When I arrived, he sat me down, looked me in the eyes, and said, "Son, what's going on?"

In that moment, time slowed to a crawl. Of course, I got defensive. "What do you mean, Dad?" I said, eyebrows curling in anger. "You know exactly what's going on."

Obviously, that was not the answer he was hoping to hear, because he stopped asking me what I should be doing and told me what I was going to do.

I was to immediately move back in with him. "Don't worry about your rent," he told me. "I'll cover your share. You're going to focus on passing the bar. We're going to do this, you and me, together."

How, I wondered, was he going to help me pass the bar?

By reminding me, he said, that I couldn't pussyfoot around anymore—that the best way to combat fear and failure is to rush headfirst into it.

So it was his house—and his rules. He woke me up every single morning at the break of dawn. He peered over my shoulder as I studied. He pressed. He pushed. He prodded. He motivated.

He dished out a lot of tough love during my stay. And in doing so, he slapped some common sense into me in the process. He broke the spell.

Next time I took the bar, I blew it out of the water and never looked back.

Cut to July 2018. Andy is standing in an airport terminal saying, "I can't do this, Darren. I'm not getting on that plane."

What could I do other than rip a page out of my dad's playbook? So I slowed the conversation down.

"OK, Andy, what's going on? What's the problem?"

All of his doubts and fears and worries came pouring out of him in such a rush that they sounded like one breathlessly long run-on sentence. "This trip has not been properly organized. We're not prepared for this. Our clients are nervous. They're not prepared. I'm not doing this. Darren, this is just not going to happen."

I started with a soft touch. "Andy, you're going to do this," I told him. "We're going to do this together. You've put in the prep. Now, it's time to see this thing through."

Based on Andy's response, it became clear to me that his fears were not going to be easily allayed. "You're wrong, Darren," he said. "We are not ready for this. This is prime-time litigation. I'm not doing it. I'm not going to put myself, our firm, and our clients in a position where we can embarrass ourselves on national television."

My eyes glanced at the clock. Every minute I spent trying to rebut Andy's concerns increased the odds he'd miss his flight. We literally didn't have time for this. Not here. Not now.

So I transformed into my father. I kept thinking to myself, "The roles have been reversed. The pupil, in this case, needed to become the mentor." Spare the rod, and thou shalt spoil the brilliant lawyer.

"Andy," I said, in a calm voice. "If you don't want to go, then you don't have to go."

This was followed by an uncomfortable pause. "What …" Andy said, "What is that supposed to mean?"

"Andy," I said, "We are pursuing a case that every lawyer in the free world would love to handle. You know what's at stake. You've spent months telling these smart, articulate, incredibly brave women that we were going to be their legal gladiators and enter the arena with them. I know you. And you know me. Neither one of us is going to be able to sleep at night if we don't step up and meet this challenge. There's no other lawyer I want leading this charge. But if you can't do this, if you decide you can't get on that plane in the next few minutes,

I promise you this: I will hang up this phone and immediately make a call to another lawyer who will."

The next sound? More pure, unadulterated silence. It lasted for what felt like an eternity.

As any of my coworkers can attest, sitting in long stretches of awkward silence doesn't bother me one bit. In fact, I rather enjoy it. Sometimes you say more by not saying anything at all. I transformed into a gargoyle; my lips became stone. I wasn't going to break. Not a single syllable. Because I learned long ago that silence, for most people, forces self-reflection.

I WASN'T GOING TO BREAK. NOT A SINGLE SYLLABLE. BECAUSE I LEARNED LONG AGO THAT SILENCE, FOR MOST PEOPLE, FORCES SELF-REFLECTION.

Push someone into a long uncomfortable silence—a witness, a spouse, or, in this case, the man I trust with our most complex cases—and they'll begin to question themselves more than they question you.

I wanted to let the gravity of the moment sink in. To allow Andy to regain his own confidence, as I did back at my dad's house so many years ago. So I waited. The seconds hand on my watch—and then the minute hand—slowly flicked around the dial. Two full minutes must have passed before Andy said, "OK, Darren. I don't like this at all, but I'll do it."

If someone yields to you, I'm a firm believer that you have a responsibility to give them something equally valuable in return. And there's no force more powerful in our world than sincere confidence.

"Andy," I said, "no one knows this case better than you do. There's no one who our clients would rather have by their side during this interview. You're a listener and a fighter. You've listened. Now it's time to fight. So just go out there and be you. That's all you have to do. *Be you!*"

And I swear all the tension that had built up between us just melted away. "I promise you, Andy. You're going to kill it," I said.

And by God, if he didn't do just that. Andy filed the suit. He staged the press conference, flawlessly I might add. He prepped all of the potential *Nightline* and *Good Morning America* interviewees for the interview. He stood by their side, in the glare of all those lights and cameras, and provided them just the guidance and support that they needed.

He cut right into the heart of the matter. Cut right to the stories, which turned out to be a cathartic experience for everyone. For many of our clients, the act of recounting their abuse to the press helped purge Dr. Tyndall's transgressions of some of their power and poison. The closest thing I can compare it to is a group therapy session. Andy and Mari created a safe space, which emboldened our clients to step forward and enact change.

It just goes to show you that confidence is every bit as contagious as fear. Support begets support. Fearlessness begets fearlessness. I remember Mari, upon returning back from the *Nightline* and *Good Morning America* taping, walking into my office and telling me, "We have to win this tort, Darren, because at this point, I feel like they're my blood, like they're my own sisters. We can't let them down."

It had been my sister who'd initially planted a similar idea in my mind back in Austin, namely that I should view these women as members of my own flock, my own congregation. Now, I realized my entire team had stepped up and accepted the role as their legal shepherds.

It was a truly gratifying moment.

The next day our firm received a call from *Good Morning America*. *GMA*'s piece aired that morning, and *Nightline* informed us that its piece would air that night, on July 23, 2018. I firmly believe that courage shown by those four interviewees to step forward and put a face and a voice to these allegations proved a critical turning point in the tort.

It was impossible for the public not to watch that segment and fail to see someone they knew—a daughter, wife, sister, friend, or coworker—in those women's stories.

They told it like it was. Amanda, a single mom from a small town, talked about the embarrassment she felt in not knowing what to do when Dr. Tyndall took photographs of her during an exam. Brennan described the confusion comingled with anger that she'd felt at being molested in plain sight of a USC chaperone. Dana, who was in a committed relationship with a woman, recalls Dr. Tyndall asking her if all lesbians hated men. And Jennifer recounted in stomach-churning detail how Dr. Tyndall rubbed his thumb against her clitoris and placed his fingers in her vagina.

It was a well-produced piece, which provided Andy an opportunity to sum up our case in just two brilliant sentences. As he told *Nightline* reporter Juju Chang, this wasn't just a story about abuse. It was a story about a university that had harbored a sexual predator for decades.

Now, all we needed to do was to wait and see how the predator would choose to respond.

CHAPTER 9

INTO THE LEGAL FRAY

There were moments during our early negotiations with USC when I assumed my eyes and ears were playing tricks on me. The denials. The subterfuge. The doublespeak. The hypocrisy. It was enough to make anyone's skin crawl.

Here are some undisputed facts, as reported by the *Los Angeles Times*.

Fact: Dr. Tyndall was the *lone* full-time gynecologist at USC's student health center from 1989 until 2017 and thus responsible for examining countless students for almost three decades.

Fact: An internal investigation conducted by the university determined that Dr. Tyndall's medical care amounted to sexual harassment.

Fact: Despite these findings, university lawyers struck a deal in 2017 with Dr. Tyndall, which allowed him to leave with a payout and a clean record with the state medical board.[11]

Fact: Despite the fact that, by mid-2018, scores of women had come forward to detail complaints of inappropriate behavior, Tyndall continued to deny any wrongdoing, going so far as to write a letter to the *Los Angeles Times*. In that note, he claimed he was aware of only one complaint, which alleged he'd failed to wear gloves during a pelvic exam.[12]

To which we, as plaintiff-side attorneys, could only say:

Goodbye, logic.

Goodbye, common sense.

So long, common decency.

The USC case wasn't my first prizefight. When you've fought your way through twelve bloody rounds with someone like BP, you learn really quickly how to weather a low blow or two.

Every bloated and soulless defendant follows the same playbook. First, they deny everything. Then they offer qualified denials: "If something did happen—and we're definitely not saying that anything actually happened—we want to make it clear that our clients are not responsible."

And then, as the defense starts to back itself into a corner, panic begins to set in. Pretty soon it becomes clear to everyone that a company's or university's reputation is on the line. So the spin doctors come out, intent on doing everything in their power to rewrite history.

---

11   Harriet Ryan and Matt Hamilton, "USC's Controversial $215-Million Settlement with Gynecologist's Victims Moves Forward," *Los Angeles Times*, February 12, 2019, https://www.latimes.com/local/lanow/la-me-ln-usc-settlement-lawsuits-former-patient-gynecologist-20190213-story.html.

12   Adam Elmahrek and Matt Hamilton, "As More Women File Lawsuits Against USC, Gynecologist Defends Himself in Letter to *The Times*," *Los Angeles Times*, May 25, 2018, https://www.latimes.com/local/lanow/la-me-usc-doctor-lawsuits-20180525-story.html.

The new directive is to rewrite the narrative. And if that doesn't work, counsel is advised to minimize the damage and write the smallest checks possible to make the problem go away.

I can't say I was surprised by USC's litigation strategy, but I had hoped for a university of its stature to show more dignity to the hundreds of their former students who were abused on their own campus.

Lawyering is lawyering. I could swallow my pride and listen to the fake news conferences. But what I couldn't stomach was the amount of additional pain they were willing to inflict on all the school's former students who'd stepped forward and tried to redress two decades' worth of lies, abuse, and embarrassing cover-ups.

Imagine the sheer chutzpah needed to imply—even if opposing counsel never came out and directly said it—that women from across the globe were either patently delusional or fabricating pain for financial gain.

Frankly, there were days when I fantasized about sitting the USC administrators down in front of a national television audience and asking them, point blank, to explain what the hell they thought had happened.

Did they actually believe that all of these women had fabricated all of these stories out of whole cloth? Were all of our clients experiencing some kind of mass psychosis? Did they view this whole episode as some kind of bizarre West Coast sequel to the Salem witch trials?

I can't imagine the anger that our clients must have felt when their veracity and integrity were called into question yet again.

Our clients could read between the lines. They were being marginalized all over again, at a time when USC—supposedly a great champion of the #MeToo movement—should have known better.

Imagine being put through that hellish rinse cycle twice. You're violated. Then, you're ignored. Then forgotten. And then dragged through the muck all over again.

During our early negotiations, things felt awfully dirty. Although this is not always the case, members of opposing counsel are known to trot out old tropes and tired stereotypes. If you're a plaintiff-side attorney, some people will try to paint your clients as money-grubbing charlatans and your team as nothing more than a band of ambulance-chasing opportunists in nice suits.

What do you do in the face of such insanity? What do you say to the traffic cop, standing in front of a fiery crash, who declares, "Sorry, folks, nothing to see here. Move along."

My simple advice? Don't be cowed into making any unforced errors. Do your job. They're challenging you to be a better lawyer. So out-lawyer them. And be willing to pull every lever of power at your disposal.

DO YOUR JOB. THEY'RE CHALLENGING YOU TO BE A BETTER LAWYER. SO OUT-LAWYER THEM.

If you have a strong case, if you have honest clients in your corner, they are going to run out of diversions and scare tactics. And when that moment does come, just lean forward and do as we did. Tell them, "Here are our demands. Take them or leave them."

Remind them that they're behind the eight ball. Recap everything: Here is what your client did wrong. Here is the evidence of what they did. And here's what it's going to cost you.

Let them know that you'll hold out as long as it takes. And should they fail to accept your clients' demands the first time around—which is a virtual certainty—explain that with every passing day, you'll dig in even deeper.

For me, the key to holding the line—and helping your clients hold theirs—lies in recalling a memory from your own past when you were made to feel powerless. Just hold onto that thought, and, trust me, the fortitude will come.

I won't pretend to know the amount of pain and distrust that our USC clients were forced to endure after their abuse. I don't know what it's like, for instance, to watch the nightly news and see USC administrators—people who willingly turned a blind eye to sexual abuse—being feted with awards and showered with adulation.

But I have experienced, more than once in my life, what it feels like to be completely powerless.

I was in the eighth grade the first time it happened. To this day, I can remember it with absolute clarity, right down to the scene, setting, and class period.

West Memorial Junior High School. Katy, Texas. Fifth period. PE class.

Picture your typical grade school gym swarming with sweaty teenagers in knee-length shorts, pumping basketballs in the air. Balls are pounding—*boomp, boomp, boomp*—against a slightly slick parquet floor. Rims are clanging. Backboards are buckling. But every so often comes a sweet silencer: a ball arcs through the air like a parabola and drops at just the right angle. *Swoosh.* Nothing but nylon.

I have many fond memories of playing basketball when I was a kid, but this isn't one of them.

I'd been enjoying a good day from the field, hitting shots all over the court. And a group of kids, huddled up near the free throw line, had taken notice. One kid in particular seemed to be eyeballing me all day. He was a big white kid—let's call him Tim—and it was obvious he didn't approve of what he was seeing.

When gym class was over and I began walking down the hallway with my friends, I saw Tim angling right for me. He stuck out his shoulder and rammed into me.

We collided, and then he reared back with both of his hands, as if he was about to give me a two-handed chest pass, and shoved me as hard as he could toward half court.

I was not as big as I am now. I stumbled, but I caught myself before taking a major spill. I wheeled around and threw up my arms, palms raised, as if to say, "What the hell was that for?"

And there was Tim, staring back at me, trying to look hard in front of his friends. He looked me straight in the eye and said, "What are you going to do about it, nigger?"

I froze in my tracks. I literally couldn't move. Although I was one of only a few Black kids in my class, no one had ever hurled that word in my direction before. I was absolutely stunned, as if someone had just tossed a flash grenade at me.

I remember hearing a chorus of snickers. The nasty kind, which are meant to inflict shame and project dominance.

That laughter hurt. Looking back, it wounded me just as much as the slur.

I remember the echo of all those squeaky sneakers—*shweemp, shweemp, shweemp*—marching along the floor. And my heart beating like crazy. *Thump. Thump. Thump.*

No one turned around to help me.

I remember thinking to myself, "What do I do now? I literally don't know *what* to do."

I felt, for the first time in my life, completely alone. All sorts of questions darted through my mind. Was I big enough and strong enough to take Tim in a fight? And if I did sprint back into our locker room and start throwing down and he beat the crap out of me anyway, what would happen then?

The shame, I quickly calculated, would be just too much to bear.

So I didn't do anything. I just stood there paralyzed, completely gutted.

As time went by, I turned my initial thoughts of pummeling Tim inward. I started punishing myself, asking myself the same questions over and over again.

What had I done to deserve that type of cruelty?

Why didn't I fight back?

How could I allow myself to be embarrassed like that?

That albatross of self-doubt and shame didn't break for a long, long time. It stuck with me—and inside of me—for years, especially since Tim and I wound up going to the same high school. He always seemed to be lurking in the distance, watching me.

I made a vow, during my sophomore year, that there was no way he was going to scar me a second time. And in making that promise, I realized that this particular story didn't have to end in the eighth grade. I could write my own second chapter and change the overall ending.

YOU CAN'T HEAL OLD WOUNDS UNLESS YOU TREAT THEM. AND YOU CAN'T CREATE CHANGE UNLESS YOU DO SOMETHING TO CHANGE THEM YOURSELF.

I tell my clients all the time that I wish karma was real. That what comes around really does go around. I wish things tended to balance themselves out in the end.

But as far as I can tell, here in the real world, that's pure pixie dust.

You can't heal old wounds unless you treat them. And you can't create change unless you do something to change them yourself.

When I was in high school, I recognized the power that Tim had over me. He didn't have to acknowledge me because he had all the power. So whenever I passed him in a hallway or shared a class with him, he'd look right through me, as if I barely existed. To Tim, I was just another invisible Black kid. A victim capable of being bullied at his whim, anytime he felt the urge.

And over time, that became a fact I could no longer accept. So I started working out more during my freshman year. I got stronger, both physically and mentally, and gained a hell of a lot more self-confidence.

Whenever I lifted or benched, I'd replay my exchange with Tim, over and over again, in my mind. I wasn't seeking revenge so much as some form of acknowledgment. I wanted him to acknowledge the scars he'd caused.

During my junior year of high school, I was presented with an opportunity to do just that. Gym class, again. Basketball game, again. Tim on one team, me on the other.

I remember Tim dribbling the ball at the top of the key, looking over the defense until his eyes rested squarely on me. He smiled. Right at me. Same look. Same smirk. Same snicker.

I know what he was thinking. He'd drive straight through me, as if I wasn't there. And I'd do what I did last time—I'd buckle and fold.

Only this time, I was prepared to fight back. I wasn't going to give an inch. My feet were so planted on that court they could've grown roots.

So he came right at me. Only there was no jelly in me this time. I was pure steel. I wasn't moving. And at the last possible moment, Tim realized what was coming. I was not going to back down. In fact, this time I was going to push his ass to the ground.

And I did. The resulting collision was so loud you could hear it in the cheap seats. He went careening off me, the ball catapulting into the air and out of bounds. And down went Tim, his body plastered on the parquet.

When he looked up, now wincing, he knew exactly who'd knocked him down. And now he was the one looking dazed and confused. I stood over him, my head curled down close to his face. I asked him, through gritted teeth, "You remember me now, don't you?"

This begs the question, Did USC remember or was it purposely blocking out the past? Did administrators remember all the complaints? The lewd photos? The chaperones who were told to leave the exams? The decades of abuse?

USC needed to remember.

Let me make one thing abundantly clear: there's no comparison to be made between being sexually abused during a gynecological examination and being humiliated in high school by some bigoted punk from Katy, Texas.

I've recounted my exchange with Tim for two reasons. Number one, I thought about that memory a great deal during our initial exchanges with USC. And number two, it's a valuable reminder that all tyrants and tormentors, no matter their age or status, tend to be staggeringly predictable. They'll keep pushing you until you push back.

Bullies will be bullies. And defense lawyers will be defense lawyers.

I've been in enough boardrooms with corrupt corporatists and craven college administrators to be able to anticipate exactly which excuses they'll make—and what lies they'll push—before they even approach a microphone.

They'll trot out every cliché in the book: We did nothing wrong. The truth will come out. Our client will be vindicated.

On and on they'll drone, reading from the same tired, clichéd script.

You know it's a smoke screen. They know it's a smoke screen, but here's the thing: Your clients might not recognize these diversions for what they are. They'll be sitting in front of their TVs and phones, hanging on to every single word.

So pick up the phone and call them. Explain what's happening. Be their translator, so they understand what's really going on behind closed doors.

In the case of USC, the reality on the ground had to be much different from the cool facade the defense was projecting in public. There had to be an expensive boardroom somewhere on USC's campus that was chock-full of high-priced lawyers sweating profusely through their monogrammed dress shirts.

Use your understanding of the system—of the legal gamesmanship that's played—to reassure your clients that they've made the right decision. Remind them that, in time, their truth will conquer any legal maneuverings that the defense might make.

That's certainly what happened once *Nightline* aired its segment on USC, in July 2018. The defense could feel the ground begin to shift and sink beneath their feet. I'm sure when they went back and took a deeper look at the materials and realized, "Holy crap, some of Dr. Tyndall's chaperones couldn't bear to be in the same room with him." Those internal testimonials coupled with additional women coming forward to lodge complaints spelled serious trouble.

When it became clear to USC that a shit storm was gaining momentum, everyone immediately scrambled for cover. "How did we get into this mess?" suddenly shifted to "How the hell do we get rid of this problem at the lowest cost possible?"

You'll know the defense is changing its strategies when lawyers start softening their language. Keep an ear out for the stammer, which we heard a lot of from USC's counsel as the case progressed. "Oh, well, gosh, um … you know … if something did happen, we want to send our sincerest apologies to those who might have been harmed."

There will, of course, be strings attached to these apologies. The script will read something like this: "Although we are disheartened to hear of the suffering experienced by students who attended our university, we do not admit to being responsible for any of these transgressions."

A spokesman will then ascend to the podium and declare that the university is taking these allegations very seriously and has already launched an internal investigation.

Promises will be made. "If we do discover issues, we will fix them. We guarantee to all of our alumni that we will make things right."

At which point, you should immediately call up their attorneys and say, "Please define for us what exactly you mean by 'make things right.'"

In the case of USC, that pretty much amounted to "How can we weasel our way out of this by paying the least amount of money possible and refusing to admit to any wrongdoing?"

As I mentioned previously, our USC clients had the choice of continuing to pursue the mass tort we'd initiated, which entitled each claimant to present her own evidence and receive her own individual settlement. Or our clients could migrate over to a separate class action suit, which was quickly gaining momentum.

It was in USC's best interests to convince as many survivors as possible to join the class action suit rather than continue on with the mass tort, especially as the details of their proposed $215 million class action settlement were announced in October 2018.

USC offered to pay $2,500 to any USC student who'd been treated by Dr. Tyndall and up to $250,000 to those who'd alleged abuse while under his care. In a letter written to USC students and teachers, interim USC president Wanda Austin wrote that she hoped this generous settlement would "help our community move collectively toward reconciliation."[13]

Our thoughts? Pure poppycock.

In my mind, it was a gutless proposal. A cheap and craven cop-out, which proved USC was still not taking these allegations as seriously as they should have.

As I've mentioned previously, we don't pursue class action cases at D. Miller & Associates, PLLC. And here, in plain black and white, was a perfect example as to why we encourage all of our clients not to either.

At this point, Tyndall remained steadfast in denying he'd done anything wrong. Given that our clients had informed us that they wanted the truth to come to light, this was a step in the wrong direction.

Why would we ever support a class action settlement that curbed our ability to take additional sworn testimony and depositions and block requests for documents that could reveal just as much as USC knew and when exactly the university knew it?

In most class action proceedings, very few depositions are taken, and the discovery process is minimal. The primary goal is to shunt plaintiffs into different classes, based on the particular type of abuse they've suffered, and then assign a specific dollar amount to each classification.

If you experienced X abuse, you will receive Y amount of money. If you experienced a different type of abuse, you will be given Z amount. And so on.

In most class action cases, a judge appoints a lawyer or group of lawyers to oversee the process. In doing so, these attorneys often rack up exorbitant fees, which dissuades them from doing everything in

---

13   Harriet Ryan and Matt Hamilton, "USC's Controversial $215-Million Settlement with Gynecologist's Victims Moves Forward," *Los Angeles Times*, February 12, 2019, https://www.latimes.com/local/lanow/la-me-ln-usc-settlement-lawsuits-former-patient-gynecologist-20190213-story.html.

their power to ensure that (A) their clients receive the largest individual settlements possible and (B) the defendant will take full and complete accountability for its negligence.

Under the class action settlement, USC experienced little more than a slap on the proverbial wrist. The university agreed to hire "an independent women's health advocate" to ensure allegations of improper sexual or racial conduct were properly investigated.[14] In addition, USC vowed to conduct additional background checks and improve employee training.

Our clients reminded us, time and time again, that they continued to be appalled by the lack of acknowledgment by USC, especially given all the evidence that had been presented to administrators.

For most of our clients, this was less of an issue of money and more about vindication. There's no doubt that hitting USC where it hurt—in its pocketbook—was one of our priorities. A financial punishment was warranted, and they told us that it was our duty to fight for the maximum settlement possible. But to a woman, our USC clients kept reiterating that they were just as interested in forcing USC to come clean and admit what they'd done wrong. They wanted someone to admit that Dr. Tyndall had violated their bodies and USC had violated their trust.

What they wanted, most intently of all, was an apology and a big fat statement in the form of a payment.

If anything, we felt the arguments being made by class action lawyers were playing right into USC's hand. Their pitch to survivors? Take what you can get, while you can get it, because nothing's guaranteed if you take this fight any further.

---

14   Harriet Ryan and Matt Hamilton, "USC's Controversial $215-Million Settlement with Gynecologist's Victims Moves Forward," *Los Angeles Times*, February 12, 2019, https://www.latimes.com/local/lanow/la-me-ln-usc-settlement-lawsuits-former-patient-gynecologist-20190213-story.html.

And that bothered all of us at our firm because it played on people's fears—the fear of having to endure the trauma of testifying or enduring unwanted media scrutiny.

It was a pure carrot-versus-stick play. USC had showed absolutely no shame in leading with a stick. They'd overlooked these women's accusations. Covered up the university's negligence. And in some cases, flat out lied.

So how were they seeking to make amends? By dangling a carrot—what we considered to be a baby carrot—in front of everyone and saying, "This is all you're going to get."

Looking back, it was a sad, meager deal, especially considering USC knew full well that if they didn't persuade enough plaintiffs to opt out of the class action and we pushed forward with our tort, they'd have to give up the whole damn carrot patch.

Many months later, I recall reading a quote from a USC trustee justifying the university's initial offer under the pretense that it was important to offer women an "easier and less impactful" way to attain some type of compensation.[15]

To which I would ask, "Easier and less impactful for whom? USC or the women who'd been under USC's care?"

I don't begrudge a single one of our clients who chose to pursue a class action settlement rather than continue on with us and the mass tort. Our responsibility, as their legal representatives, was to outline their options, including potential advantages and disadvantages of each choice, and then allow them to make their own decisions.

That being said, we made it clear to all of our clients that USC was offering them a raw deal, especially as it provided the university an opportunity once again to gloss over their negligence. We told our

---

15   Matt Hamilton and Harriet Ryan, "USC's Tentative $215-Million Settlement in Tyndall Abuse Cases Likely Just the Beginning of Financial Pain for the University," *Los Angeles Times*, October 19, 2018, https://www.latimes.com/local/lanow/la-me-usc-settlement-proposal-20181019-story.html.

clients that the class action settlement didn't send a strong enough message to other universities across the country that if they let this happen on their watch, they would have to pay a steep price.

I'm happy to say that the vast majority—almost two-thirds—of our USC clients agreed to keep fighting and move forward with our mass tort. There were a few dozen of our clients who said, "I don't want to do this. I can't do this. I'm not strong enough to do this." And we understood.

But when the dust finally settled, I think it's safe to say that most people who chose the class action path wound up being very disappointed in their decision, as the average settlement for the highest tier of that settlement came in at just $96,000.[16]

Consider what an Orange County mother who chose to participate in the class action said in 2021. "You think to yourself, 'Maybe this will pay for my kids' college,'" she said. It didn't.

"One thing I had been hoping for is to get closure," she concluded, "and what I don't have is closure."[17]

---

16   Matt Hamilton and Harriett Ryan, "For USC Women, Largest-Ever Sex Abuse Payout Leaves Bitterness, Vast Disparities," *Los Angeles Times*, May 2, 2021, https://www.latimes.com/california/story/2021-05-02/usc-tyndall-sex-abuse-settlement-leaves-some-victims-bitter.

17   Ibid.

CHAPTER 10

NEGOTIATION BOOT CAMP

FIND YOUR POKER FACE

High-stakes settlement discussions are pure poker. A variation of no-limit Texas Hold'em, where the players sport fresh-pressed suits and designer shoes instead of zip-up hoodies and bad sunglasses.

One game is played with a deck of cards and chips on green felt tables. The other in climate-controlled conference rooms atop immaculately waxed tables using pens, passive-aggressive language, and the occasional term sheet.

If you've ever played Hold'em, you know the rules. Two cards are dealt down, and five shared cards, called community cards, are flipped up and fanned across the table. Everyone can see the whole board, except everyone's two down cards. Best poker hand—or more often, the best poker player—wins.

If you've come to a point in a case when opposing counsel is actively petitioning you to discuss numbers, congratulations. The poker of face-to-face negotiations is about to begin. All the cards are likely on the table—in poker parlance, the flop, the turn, the river—and it's yours to win or lose.

At this point, there are few surprises left for either side to unveil. The odds have been calculated. Depositions have been taken. Pertinent documents have been shared. And both sides have attempted to shape the narrative—in print, online, and in front of television cameras—to strengthen their respective hands.

It's all legal gamesmanship from here on out. Will you slow play what you assume is a winning hand? Or go on the attack and chip away at whatever confidence opposing counsel still harbors? And what will opposing counsel's next gambit be? Try to ratchet up the pressure by bluffing or simply call it quits and fold?

Decisions must be made. If they do fold, are you going to try to play nice and ensure no one leaves the table completely busted? Or go for the jugular?

As far as our case against USC was concerned, "nice" had been stripped from our vocabulary months ago, thanks to all of USC's denials, its tone-deaf press conferences, and its paltry class action settlement offer.

By the fall of 2019, the tables hadn't just turned; they'd been completely flipped upside down. I firmly believed that the scales, now weighed down with new evidence, were tilting in our direction. Yet USC still believed it was holding an ace in the hole, which might convince us to take a lowball offer.

Their powerful hole card? A long-standing statute of limitations in the state of California, which barred survivors from pursuing damages more than three years after the discovery of abuse.

We'd been aware of this potential roadblock from the beginning but were encouraged by the passage of Assembly Bill 1619 on September 29, 2018, which extended the statute of limitations from just three years to a full decade.

In our minds, this was an extraordinarily positive advance for all abuse survivors in the state of California. Unfortunately, this law change did little to help many of our own clients, as the bill only applied to those who would suffer abuse going forward, namely after January 1, 2019.

Although we'd already drawn up strong legal arguments, mostly around issues related to fraudulent concealments, to work within the framework of existing law, we believed it was in everyone's interests— not only our clients but all survivors—to encourage state lawmakers to broaden the scope of these new changes.

As a Texas-based firm that lacked strong relationships with California legislators, we needed to start by doing some coalition building. Our first step was to join forces with a trusted firm in California, which had already established a successful track record of fighting for survivors' rights. We chose a firm headed by John Manly, who represented more than 180 women who'd been abused while under Dr. Tyndall's care.[18]

Some called us naive for thinking we could change the letter of the law in California. Others scoffed. Almost everyone doubted us. The gears of government, many insisted, would never creak to life quickly enough for us to find real justice for our clients. We were told that we were waging a losing battle, but I held out hope that we could quickly rally sufficient support to our side.

---

18   Matt Hamilton and Harriet Ryan, "USC's Tentative $215-Million Settlement in Tyndall Abuse Cases Likely Just the Beginning of Financial Pain for the University," *Los Angeles Times*, October 19, 2018, https://www.latimes.com/local/lanow/la-me-usc-settlement-proposal-20181019-story.html.

Had we attempted this Herculean feat elsewhere, say in our home state of Texas, I'm not sure we would have succeeded. Nevertheless, I kept the faith. We were fighting in the great state of California, one of the most progressive states in the nation. We reached out to representatives. We spent money. And we prayed on it, as I truly believed we were advocating for a righteous and long-overdue change.

The question I asked everyone was, "If not now, then when?" Every day I scrolled through my news feed and was emboldened by what I saw. Change was in the air. Everywhere.

Given all that was coming to light, could we not agree that abuse was abuse, no matter when it may have occurred? Could anyone continue to make the argument that the courts should brush aside Dr. Tyndall's behaviors and USC's cover-up because it had occurred more than two decades ago instead of just ten years ago? Where was the logic in that?

What we needed to do, I argued, was help educate a few brave change-agents in the California legislature and encourage them to double down on a problem that was an important issue to many voters in the state. Here, to my mind, was an opportunity for California to set an example for the entire nation. If someone led, others would surely follow.

HERE, TO MY MIND, WAS AN OPPORTUNITY FOR CALIFORNIA TO SET AN EXAMPLE FOR THE ENTIRE NATION. IF SOMEONE LED, OTHERS WOULD SURELY FOLLOW.

Manly and his firm shared in our sentiments, and we arranged a joint press conference. The solution to our problem—then, as during every other set of crossroads in this case—was to provide our clients an opportunity to stand before a microphone and share their stories.

We did just that. During our joint press conference, more brave women stepped forward to detail their abuse.

It was a powerful moment—so moving that members of both of our teams felt tears stream down their cheeks.

These stories caught the attention of numerous California assembly members, including Eloise Gómez Reyes, who began drafting what would become Assembly Bill 1510. In collaboration with Manly's team, Mike Arias, and members of the Consumer Attorneys of California, we worked to provide Reyes critical testimony and context, which only emboldened her and others to ensure the bill was signed into law.

By the spring of 2019, USC was clearly feeling the heat, as it hired a San Francisco–based lobbying firm to try and block these changes from ever becoming law. To add insult to injury, USC hired the same lobbyists who had fought to stall a bill written to protect swimmers from predatory practices that had previously been employed by some coaches.[19]

To my mind, this was merely a continuation of a dispiriting trend, yet another example of USC administrators doing everything in their power to prevent our clients (and scores of other women who'd been abused early in Tyndall's career) from receiving just compensation.

Was it legal? Sure. Was it the right thing to do? Absolutely not.

Fortunately, the California state assembly pressed forward and passed Bill AB 1510, which extended the statute of limitations for women who'd been abused by Dr. Tyndall.[20] In fact, that landmark bill opened the door for anyone who'd fallen victim to inappropriate

---

19   Mia Speier, "USC Hires Lobbying Firm to Oppose Legislation for Victims of Abuse," *Daily Trojan*, April 19, 2019, https://dailytrojan.com/2019/04/19/usc-hires-lobbying-firm-to-oppose-legislation-for-victims-of-abuse/.

20   Ashley Macedo, "Bill in State Assembly Forgets Survivors in Public Universities," *The Daily Californian*, June 13, 2019, https://www.dailycal.org/2019/06/13/bill-in-state-assembly-forgets-survivors-in-public-universities/.

touching or abuse at a student health center from 1998 to 2017 to pursue just compensation.[21]

Shortly after the bill was ratified in the fall of 2019, attorneys from USC began ratcheting up efforts to meet with our firm. And thus the negotiations and the high-stakes poker game began.

I've performed a great deal of mediation over the years, which requires you to ensure both parties know where the other side is coming from. You define potential impasses, summarize the strengths and weaknesses of each party's positions, and then play referee, acting as a neutral facilitator. You know you have done your job well if, in the end, neither party is extremely happy with the result.

That wasn't going to be our goal here. Our clients had told us, in no uncertain terms, to expose USC. They said, "Do not stop until you get us proper justice."

They'd come too far and listened to far too many empty promises from others for us to adopt a conciliatory stance now.

My philosophy on mass-tort negotiations is as follows: You set a Mendoza line, a minimum threshold that everyone agrees you won't ever dip below. You draw a line in the sand, and you hold that line.

In the case of USC, it came down to one simple question: How much money, at a minimum, would USC need to pay to compensate these women for the abuse they endured *plus* the negligence that USC showed in the aftermath of those abuses?

At this point, we had no choice but to advocate that our clients, on average, accept no less than seven figures each. Some might receive more, some less. But the average needed to be seven figures per client.

If we started there, the math was simple. A little over a hundred women had stuck with us as we pursued the tort. If we were to demand

21   "California '#MeToo' Bills Broaden the Scope of State Civil Rights and Sexual Assault Laws," JDSupra, October 4, 2019, https://www.jdsupra.com/legalnews/california-metoo-bills-broaden-the-26429/.

NEGOTIATION BOOT CAMP: FIND YOUR POKER FACE

an average of a million dollars per client, the total of USC's check to our roster of clients needed to exceed nine figures.

I'm a graduate of the "if you don't ask for it, you're never going to get it" school of negotiations. Everyone knows how the game is usually played. Opposing counsel starts low. The plaintiffs counter, and the merry-go-round goes round and round until someone cries "uncle."

Not here. Not this time. We'd cut out all that nonsense and present the number we expected to receive. No incremental bets. We'd just bet the pot and see what USC did in response.

In short, I refused to play the game. I refused to let opposing counsel get comfortable. We had to force them to squeal a little, and to do so we needed to hold firm, writing down exactly what we wanted in permanent marker.

And thus the negotiations—the real poker playing—began.

Don't have an inscrutable poker face? You lose. Can't read the body language of opposing counsel? You lose. Don't have the guts to go all in? You're definitely going to lose.

The first time USC's lawyers called us, seeking a visit, I told them they didn't need to bother flying down unless they had complete and full authority to write a check for nine figures.

That's what it was going to cost USC, plain and simple.

I told them straight up.

DON'T HAVE AN INSCRUTABLE POKER FACE? YOU LOSE. CAN'T READ THE BODY LANGUAGE OF OPPOSING COUNSEL? YOU LOSE. DON'T HAVE THE GUTS TO GO ALL IN? YOU'RE DEFINITELY GOING TO LOSE.

"Don't waste my time. Don't waste my clients' time. And don't waste my team's time." I repeated myself. "Don't come down here for a meeting unless you have the green light to write us a check from the University of Southern California for more than $100 million." And then I politely ended the call.

When they called back a second time, I said the same thing. And I continued to end every single one of our conversations the same way.

There were members of our own firm—and to be quite frank, other plaintiff-side lawyers working on the tort—who thought I was being too bullheaded. I remember one of our litigators coming up to me and saying, "Darren, if USC calls and says they're willing to settle our cases for $90 million, there's no way you can decline that offer."

To which I responded, "Watch me."

It's true these were extraordinarily high figures. No one had ever offered us that large of a settlement offer for a single docket of cases before. But a firm's past settlements have nothing to do with the value of the cases it's currently handling.

And that's where so many lawyers go wrong. They use their previous settlements as a frame of comparison, as opposed to standing firm on what their current cases are actually worth.

So we played the long game. USC called, and we stood our ground. Nine figures, then we can talk.

And why, you might be asking, was I so confident that they'd eventually see things our way? Because I knew opposing counsel had analyzed our track record.

There are lawyers who can win cases in court—see Andy Rubenstein—and there are lawyers who send out demand letters and quickly settle whenever the threat of actual litigation arises.

USC's lawyers could see all too clearly which camp we were in.

They recognized we had the trial experience to take our cases all the way and expose, for the entire world to see, what really happened on USC's campus. And that put the fear of God in them.

We'd put in the work, and our reputation spoke for itself. We kept an iron-tight grip on the facts, and USC recognized that if our clients testified in front of a jury, that jury box would be filled with sneers of anger and tears of sadness. And when those jurists returned from their deliberations, USC would be at risk of paying far more than just nine figures.

In the end, it always comes down to one word: risk.

How much risk is a defendant willing to take? And can that same defendant—in terms of dollars and reputational costs—afford to absorb that max pain threshold?

If the answer, to either of those questions, is no, they have to settle. And in this particular case, Dr. Tyndall and USC's actions were so egregious, and so many atrocities had been committed, that they had to fold their hand and pay up.

We had to hit USC hard with punitive damages so large that no other institution in the land would ever dare sweep this kind of behavior under the rug again.

On September 16, 2020, USC agreed to fly down to Houston and hammer out a deal. We'd agreed to a full two-day visit. We weren't being antagonistic. In fact, we spent the first night sharing a meal and getting to know each other. We pulled out all the stops. We treated USC's legal team to a night out at one of my favorite restaurants, Georgia James, in Houston.

Whenever I want to ensure a guest has a memorable night—or take my staff out to celebrate—I order the "chef's pick." It's a four-foot-long slab of wood gilded with the most expensive cuts of beef, chicken, and seafood you can imagine. Dry-aged steaks. Wagyu beef. Lobster. Pork belly. It changes daily, but it's undoubtedly one of the best meals you can order in the state of Texas. Both ridiculously decadent and outrageously expensive.

So we gorged and exchanged pleasantries. We were having fun. Not talking business at all, nothing about the case, but I was watching every move, as if I was sitting at the champions' table at the World Series of Poker. They didn't look confident to me. Even while they were enjoying dinner, you could feel an aura of fear around them.

Later in the night, when the USC case finally came up, I remember one of USC's lawyers turning to me and saying, "Well, Darren, I want you to know that we're still very confident in our position on this case."

I nodded my head and maintained my poker face. But I saw everything I needed in that moment: He was a bad bluffer. He didn't have a lick of confidence in their case.

We said good night. A late-night dinner turned into morning. And I knew exactly what to do. We'd scheduled our initial meeting for 10:00 a.m. There was no way I was going to show up on time. At the start of these meetings, it's all small talk. Everyone dances around the core issues and tries to feel each other out.

I wasn't going to give USC's lawyers the satisfaction of going through the usual motions. So I showed up, by design, almost two hours late. When I entered the room, I was greeted by a salvo of questions: Hey, Darren, what's going on? Where have you been?

All I did was say, "Sorry. I had a couple of other pressing issues to attend to." I played it cool as a cucumber, both stern and in control.

I sat down, turned to opposing counsel, and cut right to the heart of the matter. "OK, guys. Where are we at on this case?"

Cue the prepared script. "Well, we've got really good news for you," they said. "We're going to open with a $50 million offer. And by the way, just so you and your team know, that's just a starting offer. We have a lot more room to go up when this is all said and done. Our client is very motivated to get this done."

I got up from my chair. I addressed USC's side of the table and said, "I appreciate all of you flying down here. Thank you for your time, but you guys knew there was no reason for you to come to Houston unless you had nine figures' worth of authority."

Insert awkward pause. "Well, Darren, uh … well, Darren, we've got a lot of authority here," one of the lawyers said. "Don't you want to find out what that top number is?"

I told them that unless that number was nine figures, I had no interest in hearing it.

In that moment, I think I heard one of our lawyers cough so hard, I thought I'd have to give him the Heimlich. They shot me a look that said, "What the hell is this crazy man doing? He was just offered $50 million on a silver platter, and he's taking it as an insult."

Yes, I was because, of course, it was insulting. If you owned fine art or shares in a company and were offered half of what they were obviously worth, wouldn't you walk away too?

All I said, before turning to leave, was this: "I know this is a process, but no matter where you are currently at, you also know the ultimate figure you have to get to. *It's nine figures.* When you're there, give us a call."

I shook everyone's hands and exited the room.

Lord knows what was said immediately after I left, but about thirty minutes later, I received a call from Andy. "Hey, Darren, where are you?"

I told him I was on my way home.

"Home?" he asked. "What the hell? Why are you going home?"

"Because I made it clear, on multiple occasions, what our clients deserved. You guys can sit there and talk to them all day if you'd like. That's your choice. But I'm not. I am not entertaining them for another minute unless they write a check equal to or greater than the number we discussed on the phone."

I wanted USC to know, in no uncertain terms, who was holding the winning hand. We weren't going to be sweet-talked or cajoled into anything; none of those clichéd tactics were going to work. No more bluffing. We had the high hand. And everyone knew it.

Suffice to say some of my own attorneys were not happy with me. They were frustrated because they wanted the process to play out and see what number USC would end on if we kept talking. But I'd read the room. And all the players. And I knew how to proceed.

You could cut the tension with a machete over the next couple weeks. After my dramatic departure, USC's attorneys had packed up their stuff and flown home. When members of my team asked what we should do next, I said, "Nothing. We are not blinking. We'll hold service. If they're waiting by the phone for us to call them, they are wasting their time. Not going to happen."

Months passed before USC's lawyers called us back. They said, "Hey, not sure if you heard, but another firm is going to settle their cases. Here's what they're selling for."

I said, "I don't care about that number. Those are *their* clients, not ours." And I reiterated our position. We'd spoken to our clients. They'd reassured me that they were prepared to hold out for a settlement that sent a clear message.

Week after week, I just kept reassuring our team. "They are going to blink. I promise you. From what I saw and what I continue to see happening at USC, this deal is ours."

Every time I passed Andy and Rochelle in the hallway, they gave me a look that said, "You better know what you're doing." And I did. If there's one thing I definitely know, it's how to play a winning hand.

Always have, both at the poker table and in the conference room. But damn if things didn't work out exactly as I said they would.

It was early in 2021. The phone rang. I listened closely, nodded my head, and smiled wide. By March 24, 2021, a memorandum of understanding would be officially signed, effectively settling the case.

We'd won the whole damn pot.

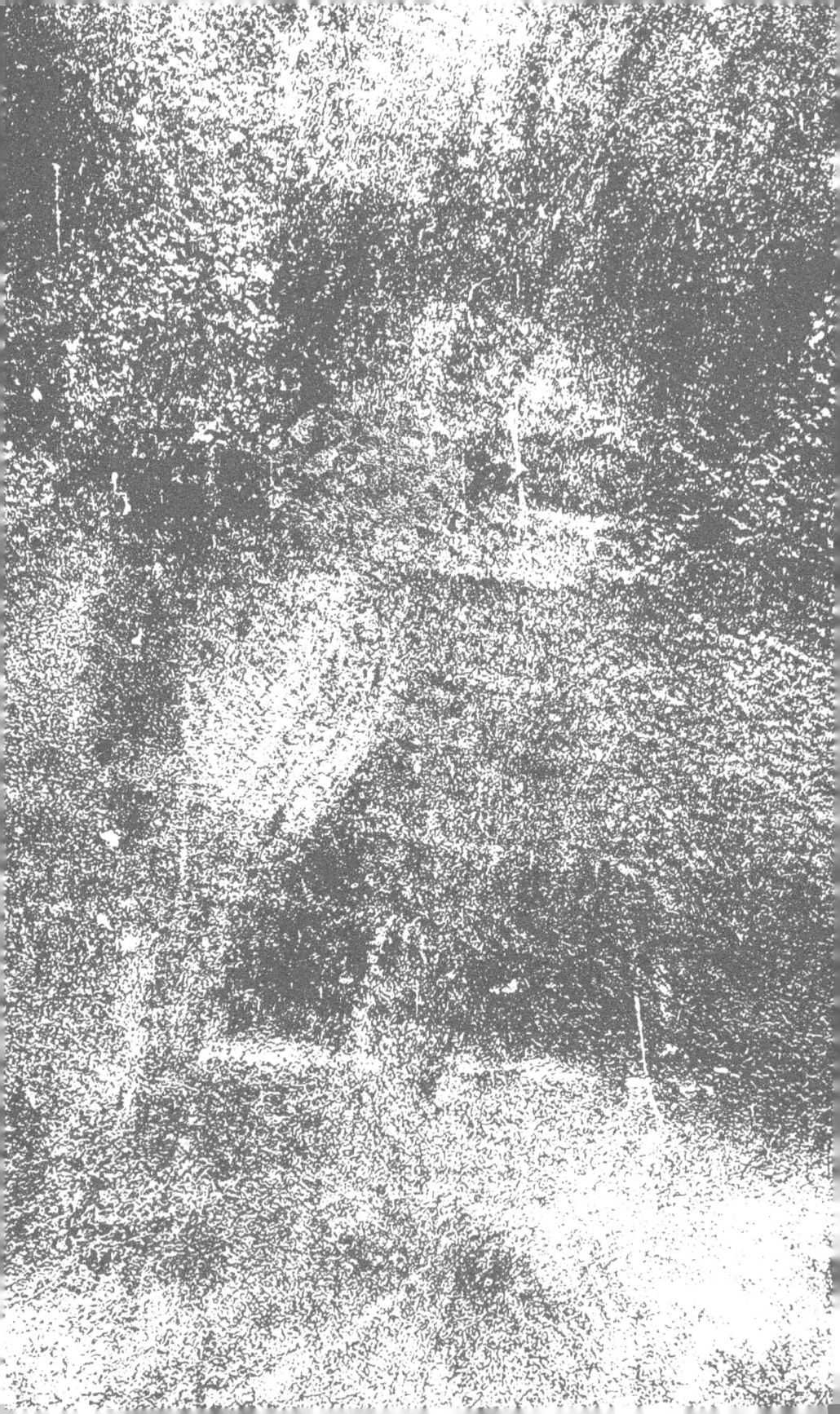

CHAPTER 11

END GAME

TO THE VICTOR GOES THE RESPONSIBILITIES

How do you define "victory"? In the legal field, the word "victory" sounds like it should be pretty cut and dry. Someone wins. Someone loses. To the victor goes the settlement. And to the loser goes one fat bill. Only it's not that simple, is it?

The older I become, the harder it is for me to formulate a suitable definition for the word "victory." True victory is elusive and very slippery, like a fresh deck of playing cards that needs breaking in.

If you're young—especially if you're young and have just earned your law degree—you probably can't help but equate victory with cold, hard cash. Money means power. The larger the settlement, the greater the feeling of true accomplishment.

For some people, that formula doesn't change very much, no matter how much time passes. I still know plenty of mass-tort lawyers who remain little more than adrenaline junkies. Folks whose sole goal, year in and year out, is to collect checks laser-printed with long strings of zeros on them.

Even after all these years, I have to admit that those checks do feel good, pure satin to the touch. It's still exhilarating to see, in physical form, the fruits of all your labors. And the act of phoning your clients to inform them that their checks are literally in the mail is an absolute thrill.

I was a young adrenaline junkie of a lawyer myself at one time. And I remain unapologetically nostalgic about the day I received my first true "mailbox" surprise.

I was twenty-eight at the time, finishing up my law degree at Thurgood Marshall School of Law. I walked to my mailbox, as I did every afternoon, to file through the usual dross—credit card solicitations, catalogs, bills—only to spot an envelope I immediately knew was no junk mail.

When I ripped it open and realized what I was holding, I swear the clouds parted and a beam of sunlight arrowed down over me. I couldn't believe my eyes. Strike up the hallelujah chorus. I was holding a check for $10,000—with my name printed on it.

Up to that point, it was the single largest check I'd ever received.

I'd worked hard for that check but had been told in no uncertain terms that there was no guarantee I'd ever receive it. For two years I'd helped a firm process a mass tort involving fake counseling centers.

If you're of a certain age, you might recall a series of TV commercials that aired during the 1990s that promised to help underachieving students and troubled teens get their lives back on track.

The ads, which seemed to air on a constant loop during daytime talk shows, played on all the usual fears that parents harbor about their teenage children.

The commercials opened with a series of open-ended questions, each ending with a simple response: Has your child suddenly begun acting out in class? We can help.

Has your child stopped communicating with you? We can help.

Have you noticed your child's grades slipping or that they've suddenly fallen behind in their schoolwork? We can help.

After being exposed to these commercials for days, some parents threw their kids into the family car and drove them down to a nearby center for a visit. In most cases, they were heartened to find beautiful manicured campuses, complete with a polite and welcoming (read: snake charmer) administrator who'd dole out *Pollyanna* visions of brighter tomorrows.

These slick counselors would promise parents the world. They vowed to help build up their children's self-esteem, improve their communication skills, and boost their grades, all while stamping out whatever rebelliousness had begun to take root in their once well-behaved young prince or princess.

This, of course, was exactly what Mom and Dad wanted to hear, so they'd nod their heads in approval, swiftly hand over their insurance information or credit cards, and sign whatever agreements were placed in front of them.

Little did they know that they were being completely bamboozled by shakedown artists masquerading as feel-good psychologists.

The minute a parent signed on that dotted line, some troll in a back office somewhere would begin analyzing Mom and Dad's insurance details to determine just how much and how long they could squeeze money out of them.

If a family's medical insurance paid for four weeks of coverage, the centers would make damn sure that their children received no less than four weeks of "treatment." If a family had a Cadillac medical plan (or plenty of expendable cash), they would prescribe months of special "treatment."

Only there was nothing special at all about the "counseling" sessions these kids were given. If anything, they often did more harm than good. Countless kids were psychologically and physically abused during their stays at these facilities.

In my eyes, these parents were paying good money to ensure their children would do hard time inside a juvenile delinquent center. Some of our clients told us horrifying stories of their kids getting hooked on drugs, spiraling deeper into depression, and, in some cases, being abused.

Whenever a parent's insurance ran out—or they were bled completely dry—the school would miraculously declare its treatments complete and assure parents that brighter days were in store for their child.

Shortly thereafter, Mom and Dad would find they were sharing their home with a far more troubled teen than the one they'd dropped off.

The firm I'd been working for at the time managed to sign up almost six hundred plaintiffs. And it was my responsibility to interview these wayward sons and daughters and write up short reports. I'd then hand off my reports and wait for the litigation to run its course.

If ultimately successful, I'd receive a check. If not, I figured it was no loss, as I'd accrued invaluable experience.

As it turned out, the firm had brokered a huge settlement, and my bonus for doing good work on this case was roughly $10,000.

It felt, if I'm to be honest, like pure magic. I'd found a case that I believed in. I'd done the work necessary to help these kids and their families. And then, *shazaam*, one day I open up my mailbox to find, much to my delight, a big fat check just waiting to be cashed.

Even sweeter than the money was the realization that I could do well for myself by doing well for others. From that point on, I knew I wanted to be a mass-tort lawyer.

And that same general sentiment—do well by doing good—continues to drive me to this very day. It's what emboldens me to take on greater and greater challenges and accept larger and larger responsibilities as every year streaks by.

If I've said it once, I've said it a thousand times. Money is a by-product of hard work. If you can develop your inner compass as a lawyer—a real unyielding sense of right and wrong—and cultivate your inner grit and resiliency, all your money problems will often take care of themselves.

> **IF YOU CAN DEVELOP YOUR INNER COMPASS AS A LAWYER—A REAL UNYIELDING SENSE OF RIGHT AND WRONG—AND CULTIVATE YOUR INNER GRIT AND RESILIENCY, ALL YOUR MONEY PROBLEMS WILL OFTEN TAKE CARE OF THEMSELVES.**

So try to do as I do. Every so often, ask yourself these two questions: Am I willing to do the right thing even though everyone around me insists that I'm doing the illogical thing? Am I retaining my faith—in my clients, my team, and the entire system—when everyone else seems to be losing theirs?

Because, at the end of the day, that's where the real glory can be found.

I remember a period of time when we were locking horns with British Petroleum in the wake of the Deepwater Horizon oil spill. It looked as though all hope was lost. If the oddsmakers were to be believed, we were going to lose our case and lose it swiftly.

I was nervous not only for our clients but also for the future of our firm.

I'd spent more money on our BP case than we'd ever spent on any other single piece of litigation before. I'd gone all in, yet all the momentum seemed to be shifting to BP's side.

It wasn't really our fault. We'd served our clients well, but a small group of plaintiff-side lawyers outside of our firm had done a piss-poor job of vetting some of their cases, and BP had used their negligence to attack every claim brought before the court.

The opposing counsel made a simple argument: if so many individual cases were this weak, then didn't it stand to reason that all of these BP suits were baseless as well?

After years of work on the case, public opinion—not to mention judicial rulings—seemed to be shifting in BP's favor. Given how much time and money we'd poured into the case, I might have taken a measly settlement—mere pennies on the dollar—just to make it all go away and hand my clients something for their troubles.

But in a way, it was my clients who provided me the strength to soldier on. Every time we called them with an update, I'd listen to how much they'd lost and would continue to lose with every passing day. Everyone reiterated how much trust they had in us, so I couldn't help but hold the line. We just kept punching. And lo and behold, by extending the case, BP wound up making a series of unforced errors.

Provide some defendants enough time and enough rope, and they really will tie themselves into knots. BP just kept screwing up. Evidence emerged that the company seemed to be paying people off. And over time it became clear that they were disregarding the science that had been presented to them. In aggregate, all this mounting evidence convinced the judge that BP, as we had vociferously argued, really didn't care at all about any of the destruction that the company had wrought.

At one point, the judge had clearly seen enough. He turned to BP's counsel and said, "I think it's time for you to settle these cases."

What an exchange! A tidal wave of emotions rushed over me. Relief. Joy. Excitement. It was indescribable. If you've ever experienced a turn of events that dramatic, you can't help but want to keep accumulating as many of those moments as possible.

When a judge makes a declaration like that, especially on the federal level, the defense has no choice but to acquiesce. If the defense doesn't yield, they're going to see some difficult rulings come their way and ultimately big verdicts handed to them over time. The alternative? Just settle.

Faster than you could say "oil spill," a team of mediators came calling and quickly worked out a deal, which provided the victims of the oil spill a long-overdue but just deal.

Over the course of the next six months, we put together a mediation and resolution plan, which culminated in us going down to New Orleans for a series of settlement conferences that eventually enabled 95 percent of our cases to settle.

I'm sure most of our clients remember the day they received their checks. But for me, the sweetest moment came when I regrouped with my team and witnessed everyone's mood shift from dread to outright jubilation.

The same exact thing happened with our USC case. After the settlement was brokered, we celebrated, as a team, all the good work we'd performed. And yes, the numbers were high enough—in total, our clients received an average of $1.2 million per individual—to make me feel like the skies had parted once again and redirected all the light in the sky into our little conference room.

In terms of USC, I am proud—and will remain forever proud—of the work we did to secure what, at the time, made the headlines as the single largest sexual abuse settlement in the history of higher education. For some of our clients, the settlement allowed them to embark on a new career path. For others, it allowed them the opportunity to seek the kind of professional help they needed to help heal some very deep wounds. Many talked about how these funds would help their children enjoy a less traumatic college experience than they had experienced.

And yet the single word that remains seared deepest in my memory is not "victory" but "vindication." I can't reiterate this point enough: out of the one hundred women who we ultimately represented in our suit against USC, 98 percent of them didn't broach the topic of money at all when they contacted us for help.

I know that might be hard to imagine, but it's the truth. These were women—highly intelligent and often very successful women—who made it clear that we needed to hold out for a large settlement, not for their own personal gain but for the message that a massive settlement would send to USC and the world.

I can't tell you how many of our clients said to me, "I want a settlement that ensures USC will be scared to death to ever allow this to happen again."

And that's what we gave them.

They'd demanded an apology, and, at long last, finally received one, along with a promise from USC that the university would draft a new bill of rights for women and sexual abuse survivors. That, in my mind, was the real victory.

When we celebrated, we were cheering the fact that so many of our clients had called us back and said, simply enough, "I feel seen. I feel listened to. I feel vindicated."

All those zeros, for them, were a means to a greater end. It wasn't the money that mattered as much as the accompanying feeling of empowerment. Winning this case helped motivate them to stop peering backward and start looking forward.

They'd changed, but we'd all changed as a result of representing them as well. I'd learned that on-campus sexual abuse isn't a single spasm of trauma; it's a systemic problem that we all have a responsibility to help fix.

At the end of the day, it's really a question of power and control. Who should gain additional power, and who should relinquish some of it? Victory comes when the scales of justice are rebalanced and new pathways are created to help young women claw back some of the power that they've ceded to others for far too long.

For me, that was the greatest reward, because that feeling of vindication rippled through every one of us. I've spoken before about how we all felt the weight of the world on our shoulders. But to feel that weight lifted and transformed into hard-earned elation was an indescribable high.

VICTORY COMES WHEN THE SCALES OF JUSTICE ARE REBALANCED AND NEW PATHWAYS ARE CREATED TO HELP YOUNG WOMEN CLAW BACK SOME OF THE POWER THAT THEY'VE CEDED TO OTHERS FOR FAR TOO LONG.

I know every member of our staff felt it too. I owe them so much. They gave all of themselves to this case. They sacrificed an immeasurable amount of energy to this quest—time they would have otherwise devoted to their spouses and families, to their boyfriends and girlfriends, to their friends and community.

I fed off their energy every single day. When you peek your head out of your office at 2:00 a.m. and see others burning the midnight oil right along with you, you quickly realize that passion and commitment are just as contagious—if not more contagious—than fear.

You hear military veterans talk about this sort of "all-for-one, one for-all" ethos all the time. You fight for the person next to you just as much as the cause itself. It might sound maudlin, but there's no greater responsibility, as the leader of a law firm, than to protect the people who've helped protect you.

I've always told my team, "If you take care of our clients, I will take care of you. You're going to want for nothing. Your problems will become my problems, which means you will have no problems at all."

I'd done my best throughout the USC case to make good to that vow. Problem with a boyfriend? Let's talk. Looking for a new place to live? Let me help. Someone giving you trouble? I'm going to come down there and straighten it out myself.

Providing bonuses and salary bumps are undoubtedly important ways of saying thank you, but providing people opportunities to grow and evolve and take on new career paths may be even more vital for their long-term success.

And those conversations with my own team members invariably turned my attention back to our clients, many of whom I now saw as extended members of our firm's larger family. "How could I help them," I asked myself, "continue to grow now that the settlement had been signed?"

I thought a great deal about Betty, who was one of the first women to come forward and inspire all of us to pursue this case. I guess it's only fitting that, out of all of our clients, Betty received the largest settlement of all.

The check she received from USC provided her financial security, but some days I wonder if we've all done enough, individually and societally, to help her feel truly whole again.

She'd been vindicated. Her truth ultimately defeated USC's lies, but how would she overcome her trauma in the long run? Would this *legal* victory ultimately translate into a long-term *personal* victory for Betty and others like her?

What's our responsibility, as lawyers, to do after a case has been won? Do we declare victory and go home and enjoy the fruits of our labors? Or work just as hard after the victory, as we did during the heat of battle?

We're committed to adopting the latter approach by hiring survivors of sexual abuse within our firm, including women like Kim Case, who have the ability to use the pain they've experienced to help others heal. I hope that other firms, corporations, and employers will join us in doing the same.

As it should be clear by now, I don't think change comes by attaining a single victory, no matter how noteworthy the result. It's created over time via a series of sustained victories—some legal, some economic, some political.

I knew, in terms of our firm, what we had to do next. We could not let this moment fade like ink on yesterday's newspaper. We had to continue to do our part to keep these women's stories and their message alive, stressing that sexual abuse was a systemic problem, one that extends far beyond any one institution, company, or abuse.

We could not accept anything less than full accountability from those who were responsible for perpetrating these horrors. This problem will never truly ebb unless we continue to expose evil, wherever it may be lurking.

I believe our message to other survivors comes down to this: You are not powerless. You can help reverse the tide, whether through your own words and deeds or by reaching out to others to help fight for you.

I know our firm is uniquely equipped, in terms of both experience and personnel, to act as their legal champions. Before the ink was even dry on the USC case, I'd already directed our team to begin pursuing other sexual abuse cases across the country.

We reached out to men who had been abused while they were in the Boy Scouts. We represented many young children, of both sexes, who were abused by clergy and various members of the cloth. We continued to uncover a staggering number of sexual abuse cases within other universities—from UCLA in the west to Ohio State University further east. Liberal areas and conservative areas. Small towns and urban enclaves. Female undergraduates and male collegiate athletes.

And in continuing the fight—and winning many of these suits—we highlighted just how much sexual abuse remains a scar on our nation and our body politic. Foolish is the person who thinks that they are immune from this scourge, because it's an evil that can affect anyone, anywhere, through absolutely no fault of their own.

So my advice after a big win? Continue to keep your ear to the ground. You want to celebrate a big win? Fine, but don't be lulled into thinking you've ever achieved enough. There's always more to do. Bathe in the bright glow of success too long, and it'll become a sinkhole that pulls you down with it.

Keep fighting, not just inside the courtroom but also outside of it. We've all heard the old saying, "True character is revealed during moments of crisis."

I wholeheartedly believe that's the case, but I also believe that character is revealed just as clearly in the wake of success. Will you safeguard your wisdom or share it? Will you hoard your money or use it for greater good? Will you accept new challenges and step out of your comfort zone or turtle away, safely within it?

So what, at this point in my life, is my own personal definition of victory? Victory is helping as many people as you can to rise above their station, whatever their station may be. That being the case, I knew I had a great deal of work left to do and knew exactly what I needed to do next. I'd won big and would aim even bigger to take on the single most ambitious and daunting risk I'd ever pursue in my life. It was time for me to enter the world of banking.

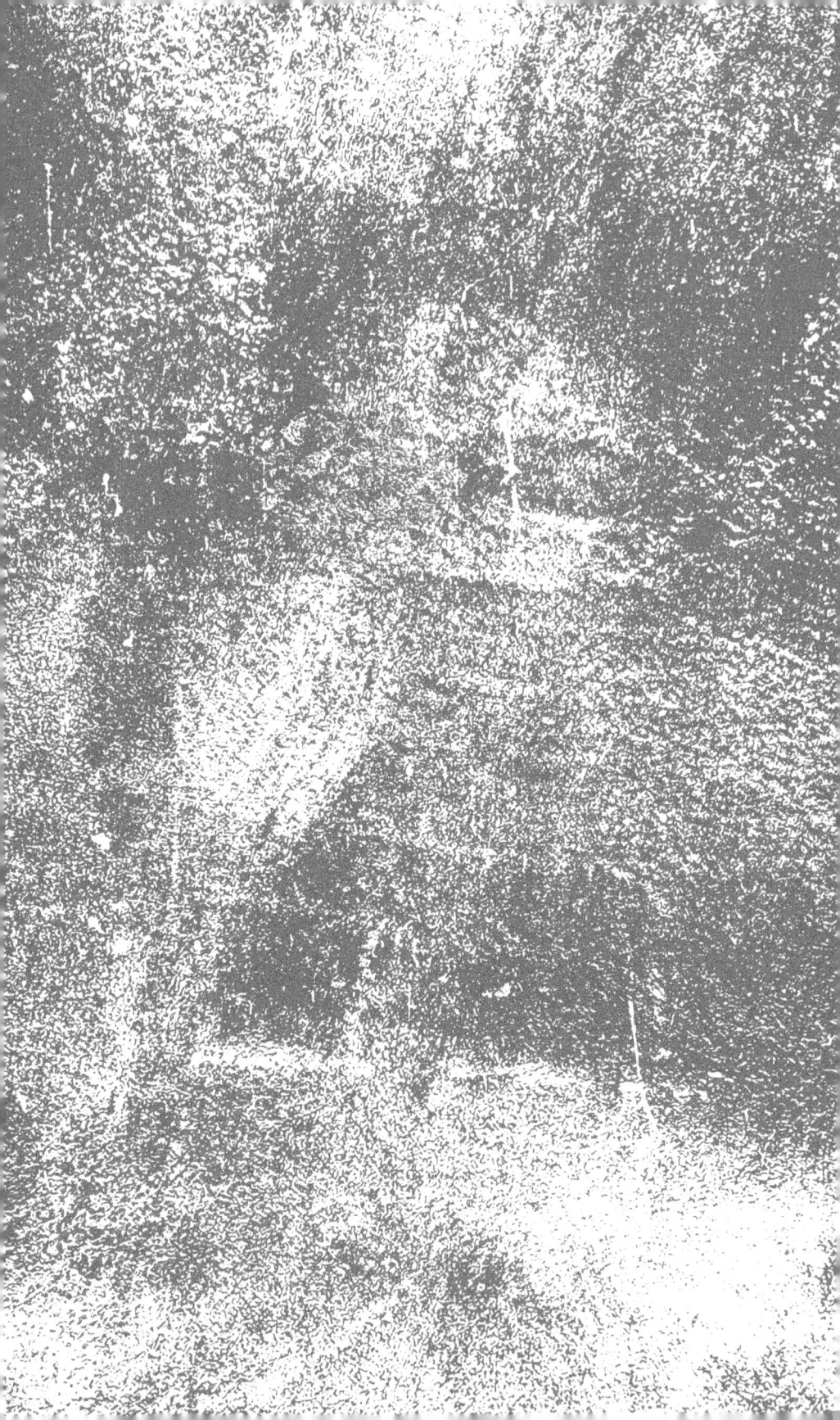

CHAPTER 12

THE PATH FORWARD

WHAT'S NEXT?

All in all, I'd say Isaac Newton pretty much figured it all out—cracked the whole source code—more than three hundred years ago. I don't give much thought to refracting telescopes, math theorems, and the immutable laws of physics, but Newton's first law is as good a business axiom as I've ever encountered in my life.

It's all right there, condensed rather neatly in a few beautifully bejeweled little clauses: *a body in motion stays in motion—and a body at rest stays at rest—unless acted upon by some other force.*

Or if I may be so bold as to slightly co-opt Mr. Newton's famous dictum: You really only have two options. It's a true binary decision. Strive or sleep. Because the minute you decide to slow down—stop reaching for that next entry on your bucket list—you're essentially on a glide path toward stasis. And the longer you drift into restfulness, the more difficult it is to regain whatever momentum you once developed.

So there you have it. Do you want to cling to past glories or seek out more ambitious ones?

I'm angling for the latter. Maybe by the time you're holding this book, I'll be able to say, with absolute certainty, whether I succeeded or failed. But over the years, I've found it's critical to at least ask yourself and everyone who enters your orbit the same question: What's next?

What do *you* dream of accomplishing next?

Let's say you're a lawyer and you've just snatched legal victory from the jaws of defeat. You just cashed a big old fat paycheck for a case no one, except your wife and clients, thought you'd ever win. Fantastic. Handshakes and high fives all around. You kicked butt. Amazing work. But I have to know, What's next?

In my opinion, the worst answer possible is to mumble the words "I don't know."

To me that's a major tell, proof that you and I see the world very differently.

By all means, take a little time for yourself. And if you don't want to reveal, for strategic reasons, what you're trying to line up next, that's understandable. But wouldn't you agree that with greater resources comes a greater responsibility to give back?

I honestly don't know what I'd do if I woke up one morning and had discovered that I had lost the desire to tackle new challenges. Just isn't me. It's not the way I was raised, nor the way I choose to live my life.

Before a single check had been mailed out by USC, I'd already moved onto other cases. An attorney from North Carolina had phoned me—remember rule number one, always pick up the phone—and we'd begun to discuss a major new case, which I'm convinced has the potential to be the largest mass-tort settlement of all time.

So I'd taken on yet another eyebrow-raising case and cultivated new partnerships, but I was also thinking beyond the courtroom too. I didn't just want to be the mind and body that stays in motion. I wanted to be that far more powerful external force that sets others in motion as well.

And how could I do that? What could trump what we'd just achieved? I had specific ideas about that—I wanted to go into banking. Actually I wanted to be an owner of a bank. A real-deal brick-and-mortar repository for people's money. I wanted to build a *community* bank that was chartered to do all the things that traditional banks do, with the added caveat that this particular bank would also cater to the needs of underserved populations around Texas.

Some people dream about building castles in the sky. I just wanted to build one right here in Houston, Texas.

A lofty aspiration? You bet.

Had I gone completely over my skis? No, I don't think so.

Was my dream achievable? Not completely sure.

Oh, but it felt right, a completely logical next step for me.

So how does one's thoughts transition, you might be wondering, from spearheading a sexual abuse suit to opening a bank?

Well, as you might have surmised, I have a deep and abiding affinity for the ignored and underrepresented among us—people of all creeds, colors, and walks of life who are ostracized by powerful institutions for simply voicing their dissent.

Our USC clients were told, in essence, that their pain didn't really matter to the university's top brass. They were told that it didn't really warrant the full and undivided attention of the administration.

Wasn't the same true for the millions of people in our country who keep our economy humming along by doing menial labor and taking public-facing jobs? Why were so many of these folks—the same people who regularly called our office for legal representation—routinely rejected for loans, mortgages, and other traditional financial vehicles?

If USC's aim was to render our clients invisible, wasn't the mainstream banking system doing much of the same for millions of others? Who was going to stand up and be their advocate? Who'd work to ensure that their needs and dreams were not completely overlooked too?

What could I do, in the wake of the success I'd enjoyed, to help empower them the way we'd helped empower our USC clients?

As I type this, my mind drifts back to the years I spent working as a special education mediator for the state of Texas. Month after month, I'd fly all over the state, on behalf of the Texas Education Agency, to help special-needs children and their families foster productive dialogues with their local districts and school officials.

I used many of the same skills that I've already recommended mass-tort lawyers adopt in this book. I phoned families, many of whom were from minority communities, and listened to their struggles. It was my job, as a neutral party, to act as intermediary between these families and their school districts. I did not represent either party. I was there as a neutral party to help facilitate discussions and hopefully broker healthy resolutions.

During these mediation sessions, there'd often be seven or eight people representing a particular school district on one side of the room—often older men or women who'd been entrenched in the system forever. And on the other side? Little old me, joined occasionally by a family member or an advocate.

Every time I walked into one of those meetings, I'd notice the same puzzled look I've described earlier when I meet with partners of white-shoe law firms. "Mr. Miller?" someone would ask quizzically, as if I'd somehow stumbled into the wrong room. "Are you Mr. Miller?"

No one would ever say aloud what I know they were thinking, but their momentary confusion spoke volumes. It said in big bold letters, "Wait a second. This guy's Black."

Nevertheless, I'd extend my hand and ask how everyone was doing. I'd exchange a few pleasantries and get down to the business at hand.

I'd begin as an outsider, but by the close of those discussions, I'd be one of their own.

Afterward, people would treat me like I was their new best friend. They'd ask me whether I'd like to stay for a home-cooked meal at their house. Or join them for a round at the local watering hole. Or swing by the local bakery with them for the best apple pie I'd ever lay my taste buds on.

It was extraordinarily rewarding work, which begged the question: If I'd already won hearts and minds within the Texas school system, why not try to do the same within the banking system?

To this day, I don't know what made me finally verbalize this dream of mine to a good friend, Sam Morris, over lunch one day. But I think my decision had a great deal to do with what I'd seen prior to our actual meal.

Sam and I meet once or twice a year to catch up and swap stories.

I have genuine affection for Sam. We're different people. We come from different backgrounds. We've pursued different career paths, which means we don't always see the world through the same lens, but it's our differences, as well as our shared values, that have forged such a strong friendship.

Prior to our meeting, I'd told Sam to meet me at one of my favorite restaurants in all of Houston, The Palm on Westheimer. I'm such a loyal customer of The Palm that the restaurant commissioned one of its famous line-drawn caricatures of me and hung it on a wall next to pictures of other prominent regulars.

Only when I drove down to The Palm that particular afternoon, I found—much to my shock—that it was shuttered. A sign informed guests not to worry. The restaurant would be relocating closer to downtown. Change, it seems, comes knocking for us all, even one of Houston's oldest and best restaurants.

So I dialed Sam and called an audible. I told him to meet me at a seafood spot not far down the street.

Only I couldn't quite shake the image of my beloved Palm, once teeming with food and drinks and lively conversation, now looking like a modern-day version of Boo Radley's house. There'd been something unnerving to me about just how quickly it had up and moved. It reminded me that we sometimes have less time than we think we do.

Over lunch, Sam and I quickly fell into our usual rhythm, picking up exactly where we'd left off the last time we met. Only during breaks in our conversation, I couldn't help but think about the ghostly remnants of The Palm haunting the now-abandoned lot across the street.

A community in motion stays in motion. And a community at rest stays at rest.

If you string enough empty storefronts together, one after the other, on a single block, it's liable to cast an eerie pall over the entire area. String enough of those haunted streets together, and you have yourself a blighted neighborhood.

Maybe, just maybe, I could do a little something to stop those dark shadows from swallowing up large parts of my own community.

So when Sam asked me the one question that I'm always asking myself, "What's next, Darren?" I blurted out exactly what I wanted to do next. I told him that I wanted to invest in a bank. Build one from the ground up and help run it. I wanted to launch a new kind of community bank. Right here in Houston.

Cut to Sam, looking so stunned you would have sworn I'd just fired a blow dart into his jugular. He all but dropped his fork onto the floor.

"Banking?" he asked, still sounding a little dazed and confused. "How long have you been planning this?"

I provided Sam a little additional background. As it happened, I'd recently begun talking with attorney Ben Crump, one of the most well-known lawyers in the country, who shared my disappointment in how underrepresented minorities were in the banking system.

My friend believed that the Biden administration would be far more motivated to address this issue, head on, than the previous administration. He'd told me that if there was ever a time to make a push, this would be the time to do it.

I told Sam that I agreed wholeheartedly with that sentiment. Now was the time to act.

Sam leaned forward in his chair, as if he couldn't wait to interject with a question. "Darren," he said, "before you go any further, if I were to ask you to outline your vision for this community bank that you want to build, could you describe it in greater detail?"

Of course I could. Despite the many so-called community banks that are currently scattered across the country, it's still rare to find many that actively encourage minority participation. At this point, I'd lost track of how many of my former clients confessed to me—even after they'd won large settlements—that they didn't trust their local banks.

They felt disenfranchised by the whole system. And what do people do when they feel like they've been denied access to a closed system? They often reject it entirely.

But that, in my opinion, was only to their detriment, as it's infinitely harder to achieve the American dream if you don't utilize the banking system that remains one of the key catalysts of wealth creation.

As I told Sam, it had always bothered me that large corporate banks didn't seem to mind that huge swaths of underserved communities had no interest in banking with them, except as a last resort. These big banks never seemed to court the kind of people that my firm has represented over the years.

I'd assumed that this was because the big banks had done the math and concluded that there wasn't enough wealth in these communities to make it worth their effort.

Only, I told Sam, that such thinking was pure folly, a mistake strikingly similar to the one that USC had made in assuming that a group of highly motivated women couldn't rise up and force the university to recognize its sins.

Why couldn't someone like me, whose parents had experienced true poverty, help rebalance the scales of power within the banking system?

More than two decades earlier, my father had loaned me $5,000 to help me start my business. I turned that small personal advance into a multimillion-dollar law firm. Perhaps, I surmised, this was my opportunity to ensure others were provided similar opportunities.

As far as I was concerned, far too many people, to this very day, lack access to something as basic as a small business loan. From a purely logical standpoint, this was not only bad business but bad for the country.

Think, I told Sam, of all the new accounts that a bank like the one I imagined could attract, not to mention all the deposits that those people's children and grandchildren might make in the years to come.

I'd always been able to do well personally by doing well for others. So why stop now? Investing in the creation of a bank, as strange as it may sound, seemed like an opportunity to learn and achieve vastly more in one fell swoop.

All Sam could say was, "Darren, I had no idea you had this dream. I never knew." But he continued on. "Look," he said, "I'm glad you shared this with me

> **I'D ALWAYS BEEN ABLE TO DO WELL PERSONALLY BY DOING WELL FOR OTHERS. SO WHY STOP NOW?**

because several partners and I are working on a potential deal to open up a new bank here in Houston. And based on what I know about you personally and the passion you've just shown about the subject, I think they'd be interested in having you become a part of this."

I told Sam, "I'd be very interested to learn more."

Here, I surmised, was an extraordinary new opportunity. An opportunity to both challenge myself and challenge others in completely new ways.

As I've noted, you can't run from risk, but you can mitigate it. When you're starting out as a mass-tort lawyer, you want to seek out more experienced lawyers to help guide you in your journey. Try to do everything by yourself, and you're sure to fail. But if you can consult with the right mentors—people you can trust and lean on—you'll never have to make a decision alone. Rather, you will make decisions in concert with others.

The exact same principle was applicable here. Change is about advancement, but it's also about gaining perspective. Change requires sharing what you've learned and absorbing what others are willing to share with you.

I was clearly ready to give and receive. To learn and educate. So in short order, Sam and his partners booked a table at an elite restaurant in Houston for our initial meeting. There were five people huddled around that table in that stunning dining room. They were all over fifty years of age. All white men.

We started talking immediately. And kept on talking the whole night through, without so much of a pause in the action. Mostly they asked me questions. Lots of questions. And I laid it all out there, my past and present, for them to ponder. What I thought and what I believed and what I was looking to achieve. I offered some personal anecdotes and hard-fought lessons that I've slipped between the covers of this book. In addition, we talked a great deal about my other businesses, some of which I've barely mentioned here.

I talked about the explosive growth of my firm. And all the other auxiliary businesses I'd created to diversify my portfolio. I talked about my real estate company, Cypress Tree Management. The intake center I launched to improve our mass-tort case processing needs. And our case-acquisitions company called DMA Advocates, PLLC, which helps lawyers who are interested in transitioning into mass torts find clients and maximize the value of their cases.

I talked about how much I'd changed. And how committed I was to helping others change as well.

And to their credit, when I came up for a breath, they didn't wait. They didn't pull the old "give us a moment to confer about this" line on me. They made an immediate proposal. "We have a very concrete plan in place," they said.

That, as you might imagine, was music to my ears. Turns out, they'd passed one of my tests without even knowing it. "We like what you bring to the table," they said. "We'd like to invite you to not only be an investor in the bank but, if your schedule allows, also be on its board of directors."

To be honest, I was a little blown away by that addendum. In that moment, I felt both validated and empowered in ways that I hope others, both my clients and team members alike, have felt at the close of various torts and cases.

As the lone Black man sitting around a table of seasoned bankers, I was clearly playing the role of the outsider once again. But if I'd learned anything over the years, it's that it's often the outsider who can engender real and lasting change. It's the outsider—who comes ready to leverage their history, experience, and unique life story—who can actually make a difference.

Everything in my life, up to this point, seemed to be leading to this moment. The values and work ethic that my parents had instilled in me at such a young age. The stories they'd shared about their struggles and triumphs. The many hours I'd spent in church pews and basketball courts and school classrooms. My time in London and New York and Katy, Texas, and Texas A&M, St. Thomas, and Thurgood Marshall School of Law. All those frustrating months spent under the thumb of oily lawyers. As well as the advantages of partnering with brilliant, caring ones as well.

I thought about all the time I'd spent building my team and fighting on behalf of my clients in the courts. All those cases, large and small. And my commitment to continue diversifying my dockets and business interests. And, of course, playing a small but passionate role in trying to expose and root out sexual abuse wherever it found shelter.

This brings me to one of the most important lessons I've learned during my journey. In the end, success comes not from money or fame or public adulation but by refusing to forget who you are and where you come from.

I have plenty of people in my life—my longtime director of personal injury, Betsy Deleon, comes to mind—who keep me grounded. But no one keeps me in

IN THE END, SUCCESS COMES NOT FROM MONEY OR FAME OR PUBLIC ADULATION BUT BY REFUSING TO FORGET WHO YOU ARE AND WHERE YOU COME FROM.

check and inspires me more than my wife, Comfort Miller.

Throughout my life, my wife has made more sacrifices than I can ever put to paper. But perhaps the most important gift that she gives me, especially when times get tough, is to look me straight in the eyes and say, "Be true to yourself, and it will happen."

I sincerely hope this is the message that I've passed on to you with this book: Be yourself. Refuse to make excuses. Take the leap. And it really can happen.

If it did for me, a kid from London who dreamed of becoming an American lawyer—a kid who moved to New York, found his way down to Katy, Texas, and up to Houston—what in the world is stopping you from chasing down your dreams too?

The answer? Absolutely nothing—nothing but time, commitment, and drive. The drive to achieve your goals.

Some months later, when my partners and I sat down to meet with a panel of representatives from the FDIC and the Texas Department of Banking to present our proposal, I didn't just bring stats and numbers and talking points with me. I brought all of myself and all of my history into the meeting as well. I shared the same ideas, philosophies, and stories that I've tried to communicate in this book. I spoke a great deal about listening and the importance of placing the needs of others above your own needs.

I spoke about the trust that's created when people speak to each other face to face. I talked about the importance of building long-term relationships and keeping the faith—faith in myself, my peers, and building a better system. And I spoke about the importance of conveying ideas through stories, of never being satisfied with the status quo, of fighting the good fight, even when the odds seem to be stacked skyscraper high against you.

I talked about how I'd learned to be a better lawyer and how those lessons would help my partners and I build a better, more equitable bank. But mostly I talked about change. How change isn't about a single person, a single case, or a single bank. Change, I insisted, requires partnerships. Lawyers. Journalists. Business leaders. Politicians. Government officials. Disparate groups of people who bring different skill sets and experiences together in order to breathe life into a larger movement.

I closed that meeting with a simple analogy. "Change," I said, "is an investment, a series of small deposits, which help us ensure that our lives, our communities, and hopefully our world will become a little brighter—and a little better—than the way we found them."

It is my belief that if my clients are a little more enriched, my staff is a little more knowledgeable, and I live my life in a way that God wants me to—by treating others with empathy and respect—then I can truly say I have done my job. That I've helped change the game. And done so to the very best of my God-given abilities.